Talking Shop

Talking Shop

AUTHENTIC CONVERSATION
AND TEACHER LEARNING

Edited by Christopher M. Clark

FOREWORD BY D. JEAN CLANDININ

Teachers College, Columbia University
New York and London

Published by Teachers College Press, 1234 Amsterdam Avenue, New York, NY 10027

Library of Congress Cataloging-in-Publication Data

Talking shop : authentic conversation and teacher learning / edited by Christopher M. Clark ; foreword by D. Jean Clandinin.
      p.   cm.
    Includes bibliographical references and index.
      ISBN 0-8077-4031-4 (cloth : alk. paper)—ISBN 0-8077-4030-6 (pbk. : alk. paper)
      1. Group work in education.   2. Teachers—In-service training.   3. Professional socialization.   I. Clark, Christopher M. (Christopher Michael)
    LB1032 .T32   2001
    370'.71'55—dc21   00-047682 .

ISBN 0-8077-4030-6 (paper)
ISBN 0-8077-4031-4 (cloth)

Printed on acid-free paper
Manufactured in the United States of America

08   07   06   05   04   03   02   01   8   7   6   5   4   3   2   1

Contents

Foreword

WHEN CHRIS CLARK invited me to write the foreword for this book, his invitation came out of a long narrative history of shared interest in teacher knowledge and teacher education. The threads of our shared narrative history connect back to my reading his and Bob Yinger's work. From that beginning, the threads twist forward to meeting when I was a student at OISE and he was invited as external examiner for Freema Elbaz's doctoral work. I knew then we shared a passion for reimagining ways to work with teachers from a standpoint of teacher knowledge.

Years later, as a new faculty member, I invited Chris to the University of Calgary to participate in a conference on collaborative research. Again we talked about teacher knowledge and rethinking professional development in terms of teacher inquiry. By then I was working with teachers, both experienced and preservice, in conversational inquiry groups. He was interested in what I was doing and we shared stories about possibilities for this work.

Still later, we met at the University of Alberta when Chris was external examiner for June McConaghy, whose research focused on the experiences of a teacher research group. Later, Chris returned as a distinguished scholar to work with a group of teacher researchers interested in participating in a conversation group. Debbie Schroeder was, at that time, engaged in another teacher conversation group as her doctoral study and she joined with Chris in the group. Chris shared stories of other researchers interested in similar work, researchers like Lynne Cavazos, whose doctoral work was with a teacher inquiry group. Lynne visited the University of Alberta and we shared stories of possibilities for linking teacher education with teacher conversation groups. I visited Michigan State in 1993 and spent time with Chris, Susan Florio, and participants from a conversation group.

The narrative threads of connection wove into the mid-1990s. By then Chris knew of enough people engaged in similar research with teacher inquiry groups to help us connect with each other. Chris began to imagine new possibilities for linking the work of these diverse groups. Many of us had figured out what happened when teachers came together in teacher inquiry groups. When teachers told their stories and responded to others' stories in sustained conversation groups, they came to understand their own practices in new ways. Their participation in these groups led them, many said, to new insights, new restoried knowledge. They reported that their practices changed. Many described their experiences in these groups as their most powerful professional development.

Chris wondered about the possibilities for asking researchers connected with such groups to engage in an electronic conversation. If the stories of the groups were placed side by side, perhaps some experiences would resonate with others. Perhaps we would see something about why such groups were powerful forms of professional development. Chris's imagination and knowledge of people working in similar ways linked us together. This insightful book is one of the results of the links that Chris fostered as he brought us together to think about teacher knowledge, teacher inquiry, sustained conversation groups, and professional development.

This book tells stories of some of the groups that formed the network. Each chapter is a detailed description and analysis of selected facets of a group's experience. Together the chapters show us the range of possibilities for teacher conversation groups, from groups of beginning teachers, to mentor teachers, to women science teachers. The groups met in the context of courses, of shared interest in subject matter, of shared work. The groups met for periods of one year to many years. Yet while the groups are extremely diverse, as are the researchers' accounts of them, there are common features that link the work.

In the final chapter, Chris looks across the accounts and pulls out seven learnings about the conversation groups. He identifies seven qualities of good conversations he saw in the chapters. In and of themselves these seven learnings and seven qualities are not exotic. As I read them, I thought, I know this. What makes the book remarkable is that readers can look back and see for themselves how these qualities are lived out in diverse groups that shared common intentions and purposes. The book shows the experiences of the groups in compelling ways that let readers see for themselves the possibility for sustained teacher conversation groups as professional development. It is a remarkable book that allows all of us to begin to reimagine teacher education.

D. Jean Clandinin
Centre for Research for Teacher Education
and Development
University of Alberta

Talking Shop

CHAPTER 1

Conversation as Support for Teaching in New Ways

Christopher M. Clark &
Susan Florio-Ruane

B EING A GOOD TEACHER is more difficult today than ever before. Social, political, and economic conditions at the beginning of the twenty-first century combine to make public education highly contested ground. Schooling is at once labeled the cause of social problems and, potentially, the cure. Cynical politicians and some sectors of the public blame educators for not fixing the many side effects of economic and social poverty: low literacy and high dropout rates, truancy, child nutrition deficits, teen pregnancy, poor performance on state-mandated achievement tests, school violence, social alienation, and disengagement from the values undergirding schooling in the United States. Meanspirited reforms of the American welfare system have effectively criminalized being poor and a full-time single parent, undermining much of the potential support teachers might realize from home. The charter school movement and schools of choice voucher programs may seem, from a public school teacher's point of view, like threats to skim away the most capable, mobile, and ambitious children and teachers, and leave the most needy to fend for themselves, with proportionately fewer resources. Teachers and children have been murdered on school grounds in communities both rural and urban, middle class and economically disadvantaged; the felt sense that school is a safe place, even a sanctuary, has been badly eroded.

All this notwithstanding, there are forces of idealism and hope at work. Writers produce inspiring accounts of education in communities where learning thrives despite limitations such as those described above (Kohl, 1998; Lightfoot, 1983; Palmer, 1998; Rose, 1995). In addition, the activism of educators and parents in some of our most economically depressed communities has inspired teachers with a sense of the moral imperative of effective literacy education for all (Edwards, 1989). Although the United States still struggles to have a productive national dialogue about race and racism, and many people of diverse backgrounds still live in extreme poverty, our explanations of and solutions to the problems of educational inequality are becoming more richly complex (Greene, 1994).

A new wave of immigration in the United States, from southeast Asia since 1975, from Central America and Mexico beginning in the 1980s, from eastern Europe and the former Soviet Union after the fall of the Berlin Wall, has been accompanied by a third wave of the civil rights movement, challenging both the social melting pot metaphor and the educational wisdom of court-mandated busing and numerical criteria for enforcing racial integration in schools. Inequitable school financing schemes that for generations have kept wealthy schools wealthy and poor schools poor are being challenged in the courts and in state legislatures. Culture and multiculturalism are being rethought and retheorized not as limiting conditions creating borders that separate people, but as processes of identification that are open to transformation over time and with increasing boundary-crossing contact.

Even as these apparent turns away from large-scale government engineering of education have produced some troubling policies that seem unproductively to turn back the clock (e.g., recent propositions that have canceled affirmative action), they also lead to promising innovations in how educators and the communities they serve participate in the management of their own learning communities. We are seeing experiments with local dialogue as a form of school governance, and historic reliance on technical management, especially in large urban districts, is giving way to bold experiments in site-based management that places teachers, students, families, community leaders, and administrators in consequential dialogue about education.

Thoughtful arguments about language usage, dialect, bilingual education, and the moral and political superiority of standard English have begun to raise public consciousness about the complexity and significance of language as the medium of learning, subject matter of instruction, and marker of cultural identity among schoolchildren and their families. Feminist theorists and cognitive psychologists have gathered persuasive evidence that ways of knowing differ in important ways for girls and boys, women and men. Computer technology and Internet access have begun to connect children and teachers in local settings to people and worlds unimagined just a few years ago.

CHANGES IN THE CLASSROOM

Progressive theories of learning and approaches to teaching grounded in the social constructivism of Vygotsky have been developed during the past 2 decades that empower both teachers and schoolchildren in personal and cooperative sense making. The idea that a school class can become a cooperative learning community rather than a competitive aggregation of separate individuals is gaining wider acceptance at every level, from preschool to graduate school. Strides are being made in the functional integration of curricula in science and mathematics, history and the arts, writing across the curriculum, and more. The blessing and curse, "may you live in interesting times," applies very well to teaching at the turn of the twenty-first century in the United States. It is indeed an interesting time to be a teacher, and it is also a bit overwhelming.

Whatever one's positions might be on particular issues in this swirl of contemporary attention and change in education, one thing is clear: Teachers are being whipsawed by a mixed message that says, on the one hand, "You are reflective professionals and moral agents, capable of and responsible for designing, studying, and refining your teaching so that all students will learn and succeed." On the other hand, an equally strong voice claims that "many public schoolchildren lack the intellectual and social capital to succeed. Lower your expectations, for it is a waste of energy to try to overcome social forces beyond your control." Indeed, the minds and morale of America's 3 million public school teachers may be the most contested ground in all of education, and the social cost of apathy and despair prevailing is beyond calculation.

CHANGES IN PROFESSIONAL DEVELOPMENT

Like the education of youngsters and the administration of schools, the continuing education of teachers seems in the process of some transformation. Teachers historically taught as they were taught—and they were taught primarily by being told by experts from outside the classroom (and school and community) what to do and how to do it. As we have moved to incorporate into our teaching and the management of our schools opportunities to learn that are more dialogic and meaning-centered, teachers have begun to be interlocutors in the process of their own learning and professional development. Work in the small spaces—those peer groups where a problem can be hashed out or an interest pursued—is beginning to be illuminated. Children are talking with peers and more experienced learners about ideas; parents and community leaders are invited into dialogue with teachers and administrators about the ends and the means of education. And teachers are being afforded time and space for talk about their work. Whether face-to-face or on line, teachers are beginning to create and sustain conversations about their profession.

This book is about what the chapter authors have learned from a set of research and development projects aimed at supporting teacher learning and development in tumultuous times. Universal uncertainty, rapidly changing circumstances, and locally distinctive challenges call for a fundamental redesign of approaches to teacher professional development and lifelong learning. The core idea of these research and development projects is that sustainable professional development for teachers must be led by teachers themselves and be intrinsically satisfying, voluntary, and inexpensive. We have begun to develop and study models for encouraging and sustaining teacher learning and inquiry in local contexts that have these properties and show promise to evolve to meet local needs for teacher learning, teacher research, and teacher-directed professional development.

In addition to the research on sustainable teacher development at sites in the United States, Canada, and Israel, the chapter authors have been in regular communication with one another via e-mail and annual face-to-face meetings since 1996. Our conversations have led us to propose a theory of how teacher talk, conversation, dialogue, and narrative can work to promote teachers' learning to teach in new ways, maintaining their essential idealism and optimism, and continuing to learn from experience in confusing times. This book, then, presents the outline of a grounded theory of teacher learning through conversation.

FRUSTRATIONS OF CONTEMPORARY TEACHER DEVELOPMENT

The history of teacher development efforts is mostly disappointing and ineffective for four interrelated reasons:

1. *Ownership.* Most teacher development programs and projects are designed and imposed from outside the professional community of teachers. No matter how cleverly these programs are designed, when teachers are not involved in framing the goals and means for their continuing professional education, they naturally feel put upon, manipulated, and not taken seriously as professionals. Researchers on teacher development frame this as the problem of "ownership" and conclude that when teachers do not "buy in" to an inservice training program, it is doomed to fail.

2. *Deficit model.* The term *teacher development* is used frequently as a euphemism for fixing what is wrong with teachers—inadequacies of skill, knowledge, technical expertise, values, and attitudes. The model underlying contemporary professional development is a hybrid of the medical (diagnostic-prescriptive) model and the troubleshooting model of electronic systems repair, in which teachers are cast as diseased or defective components in an otherwise excellently designed learning production and control system. This model (when applied to either teachers or pupils) fails to tap the learners' existing knowledge, skills, and interests as resources for continued learning (Griffin, 1991). Further, a deficit approach is antithetical to the current move to site-based management of schools, in which teachers' voices are essential for leadership in changing the conduct and ethos of schooling (Little, 1993).

3. *Contextual insensitivity.* For reasons of efficiency, replicability, and control, many inservice training and professional development programs have been standardized, that is, designed and refined so that they can be delivered in a predictable and replicable form in many different school settings. The unintended but pernicious side effect of this generic, one-size-fits-all approach is that typical inservice programs do not fit any particular school faculty well, and rarely are flexible enough to embrace and capitalize on unique local strengths and unforeseen opportunities (Darling-Hammond, 1994).

4. *Short-term thinking.* Typical professional development programs for teachers are brief in duration and intended to solve well-defined problems whose solutions can be evaluated by the end of the current school year, or even by the end of a half-day workshop. A teacher development program, then, can become a series of loosely related stabs at quick-fix solutions to narrowly defined problems. But persisting problems of practice and professional

dilemmas may require several years of building toward solutions and striking a more educationally responsible balance between, for example, the needs of the most gifted students and of those farthest behind. Long-term experiences are especially important when teachers are attempting to improve their knowledge and skills so that they can teach in ways supportive of children doing complex reasoning and higher-order thinking.

Fine-tuning and tinkering with existing models of staff development such as these is a waste of time and money. The time has come for a radical shift in thought and action in support of sustainable teacher learning and teacher research. This shift is needed to engage teachers as reasoning and responsible professionals in the process of refining their knowledge, skills, and dispositions to teach in new ways that support pupils engaging in higher-order thinking across the content areas, and to empower teachers to assume leadership in the management of schools.

PROFESSIONAL DEVELOPMENT AND INQUIRY GROUPS

Since 1994 we have established and documented the life histories of Professional Development and Inquiry Groups for teachers. The fundamental and most important goal of these groups is to change local cultures of teaching so that school faculties can become "learning organizations" (Argyris, 1991; Little, 1989). To the extent that we and the teachers have been successful, Professional Development and Inquiry Groups could become a central element of a new infrastructure for teacher learning, professional development, and adaptation to dramatically changing conditions in K–12 education.

Forms and Functions

The Professional Development and Inquiry Groups described in this collection are voluntary groups of six to ten teachers who meet regularly (weekly, bimonthly, monthly) to pose and pursue teaching problems together, and to provide intellectual and moral support to one another. This social and intellectual work is done by means of conversation that includes personal narratives of teaching experiences. We call this form of discourse "authentic conversation" (Florio-Ruane & Clark, 1993). The majority of group members are women, reflecting the demographics of the teaching profession. Although the groups are open and seek diversity in their membership, maintaining positive relational dynamics, a characteristic of women's ways of knowing, is a high priority in these inquiry groups (Belenky, Clinchy, Goldberger, & Tarule, 1986). Most of these groups meet on their own time, often in a member's house or apartment, sharing a potluck-style meal. All of the groups with which we have experience were initiated by university researchers in cooperation with local public school teachers or, in two cases, evolved from graduate courses for teachers.

Beyond these commonalities are many variations. Some groups studied were for secondary teachers only (Cavazos, 1994; Swidler, 1995; Zellermayer, 1995), others were for prospective and experienced elementary teachers (Florio-Ruane & deTar, 1995; Rust, 1997), and still others were mixtures of the two (Featherstone, Pfeiffer, & Smith, 1993; Pfeiffer, 1998). Most groups drew members from different schools and districts; in some, members were from a single faculty. Original topics of common interest showed great variety: constructivist teaching of math (Featherstone et al., 1993; Pfeiffer, 1998); process writing (Zellermayer, 1995); women's experiences as science educators (Cavazos, 1994); democratic teaching (Swidler, 1995); literacy and cultural identity (Florio-Ruane, Raphael, Glazier, McVee, & Wallace, 1997); mentoring beginning teachers (Bilelli, 1995; Orland, 1998); creating inclusive communities to integrate special needs students into regular classrooms (Schumm & Vaughn, 1995). The common thread that relates these topically diverse groups is that all of the members are actively working on professional change in their lives outside the group. The ideal Professional Development and Inquiry Group is not only a satisfying end in itself, but also a medium of support, advice, sense making, and encouragement for teachers to continue to learn how to serve their students better. One indicator of the sustainability of these groups is that, in every case in which an initiating research project or course has been completed, the participating teachers have insisted on continuing to meet, pursuing their own professional development agendas. Another indicator of sustainability is that, once groups acquire an identity, their membership may grow or change, but new members are mentored in the process of teacher development by more experienced ones. In all cases, the aim of these inquiry groups is a radical shift from control of topics and agenda by university-based teacher educators exclusively to control by teachers or by a partnership of members from both groups.

THE NEED FOR RESEARCH

The studies begin to illustrate the variety of forms and functions of Professional Development and Inquiry Groups. The researchers have documented the histories, social and linguistic dynamics, and personal costs and benefits of these groups as sites for teachers' professional development. We mounted a series of descriptive-analytic studies of Professional Development and Inquiry Groups that illustrated and refined the concept, explored the limits of the groups' versatility, analyzed the true costs of this approach to professional development, and produced case studies and cautionary tales helpful to educators who might start groups of their own. The most general and potentially far-reaching result of this program of research will be to develop a model of a new kind of professional development: a conversation-based framework that local groups of ordinary teachers can use, modify, and adapt to suit their changing needs as learners and educational leaders. The time was right in 1996 to begin building on both parts of this corpus of relatively separate field studies by adding the power of cross-site comparisons and the synergies that come from group networking through e-mail and other more traditional forums (conferences, site visits). The chapters that follow are the fruits of this cross-site synthesis of lessons learned about how conversations among teachers can serve continually changing transformative ends for teachers in a postmodern world.

RESEARCH AND DEVELOPMENT THEMES

Our original conception of this project cast it primarily as a development project and secondarily as a research project. By "development project" we meant that our greatest accomplishment would be to figure out, in context, how small groups of teachers could best begin and sustain learning conversations that made positive, powerful, and flexibly evolving contributions to their learning, teaching, and morale. These successful, long-term Professional Development and Inquiry Groups might start out looking similar to one another in form, function, rhythm, and general goals and aspirations. But we hoped they would evolve and diverge from one another to fit the unique opportunities and constraints of local situations, distinctive teacher personalities, and social and educational changes that are unpredictable in principle. The project would develop grounded answers to questions about group size, meeting formats and locations, frequency and duration, opening and closing rituals, members' commitment to learning and change outside group meetings, membership and leadership patterns, vital signs of success or crisis, and social and communicative pitfalls, to name a few of the practical matters that teachers would need to deal with in starting and maintaining such groups. The development function of the project also would include an element of persuasion. That is, our purposes would be to develop a framework for thinking about enhanced professional learning and also to convince teachers, teacher educators, and school administrators that doing this kind of professional development work is worthwhile, satisfying, and urgent. Our persuasion goal would be served through written case descriptions of group meetings over time, testimonials by teacher-participants, and honest enumeration of costs and benefits.

RESEARCH AGENDA

Loaded as this development agenda was on the side of the practical and the pragmatic, it still provided many basic research opportunities. Thoughtful self-study of Professional Development and Inquiry Groups has begun to contribute to empirical knowledge and understanding of interrelated theoretical issues, including the psychology of learning among adult professionals, the sociolinguistic dynamics of learning-oriented groups, and the forms and functions of personal experience narratives in personal/professional discourse.

The Psychology of Learning Among Adult Professionals

The overwhelming preponderance of what the field of educational psychology has discovered about human learning is situated in K–12 schools and traditional school learning tasks. Different theoretical perspectives frame competing branches of the literature on learning (e.g., behaviorist, information processing, cognitive-developmental, social constructivist). Yet the fact remains that virtually all of what researchers claim to know about how learning works is grounded in studies of schoolchildren interacting with teachers and text, within a neobehavioral transmission model of school teaching and learning. Unfortunately, this theoretical and empirical corpus serves as the metaphorical foundation for thinking about and designing inservice learning/training experiences for professional teachers. The metaphor breaks down quickly under examination: Teachers are not children; traditional school tasks are inadequate models for the uncertain, complex intellectual-practical-moral-emotional life spaces of adult professionals; traditional measures of learning (objective tests, grades, credit hours) likewise miss the mark in reflecting what and how much teachers have learned in support of their own developing professional competence. And forward-thinking educators now advocate more social-constructivist ways of thinking about school teaching and learning, with understanding of subject matter and phenomena displacing content coverage and rote recall of facts and procedures.

In brief, it is time for educational psychologists to begin anew, observing, describing, and theorizing about how learning works for adult professionals (particularly teachers) living and working in complex professional contexts. Some promising beginnings have been made in this direction. Clark (1995) has theorized that adult professional learning is predominantly "remembering, reinterpreting, and reorganizing" knowledge and skills rather than adding new information or practicing new behavior. Pfeiffer (1998) and Featherstone, Pfeiffer, and Smith (1993), in studies of teachers learning from experience, working together in one version of a Professional Development and Inquiry Group and trying to teach mathematics in a challengingly new way, discovered that the relational and emotional aspects of teacher learning are at least as important as the substantive and the technical.

Of the many informative research questions that could contribute to a practical theory of learning among adult professional teachers, we began by asking:

1. What do teachers learn from active participation in Professional Development and Inquiry Groups?
2. How are teachers different, in mind, morale, and behavior, after weeks, months, and years of authentic conversation with peers?
3. What counts as worthwhile learning and development of adult professional teachers?

These questions could have been answered years ago by armchair theorizing, by speculation, or by generalization and extension from the literature of learning research on laboratory animals, schoolchildren, or college undergraduate research subjects. Instead, we pursued answers to these basic questions about teacher learning via direct observation and participation with teachers in their learning, documentation, and description of individual and collective changes in what these teachers know, understand, can do, and feel. The teachers with whom we work are vital informants and co-investigators in pursuing these questions. Their testimony, claims, and examples of learning are primary data for our collective interpretations.

Sociolinguistic Dynamics of Learning-Oriented Groups

Fundamental to our own research on sustainable teacher learning is the idea that teachers working together to frame and solve education-related problems constitute a powerful kind of learning in its own right. Opting for a dialogic rather than a transmission-oriented approach to professional education for teachers mirrors current developments in the psychology of learning and parallels what teachers are now learning is best for educating youngsters in their classrooms. In both cases, however, we still know relatively little about how conversation about ideas and experiences supports the development of higher-order reasoning or increases knowledge (Burbules, 1993).

Our network affords several sites and opportunities to study the relationship between conversation and learning. First, at each local site, participants track the dynamic interaction of conversation and learning as part of their documentation of teacher development activities they are undertaking. Second, meetings of the group organizers at two forums each year since 1996 included time for cross-talk about the dynamics of learning conversations and comparison and contrast across the settings. Of focal attention were the strengths and limitations of conversation-based learning for teacher development. Third, the local groups have been connected via the Teacher Development and Inquiry Group electronic list, on which project members can participate in on-line conversations. These exchanges shed light on the development of conversations locally.

Among the issues studied in these rich conversational environments are the following:

1. In what ways is conversation among peers a robust medium for addressing difficult problems of theory and practice?
2. What is the nature of the talk that occurs in these groups and how is it related to learning? What role does resistance play?
3. What roles are played by procedural talk, argument, personal narrative, and other forms of talk as participants undertake their work over time?
4. What are the relative strengths and weaknesses of conversation as a basis for teacher development?
5. What is the relationship between talk within a group and the agenda for change that individuals are pursuing outside the group?

Pursuing these questions has added to our knowledge about new forms and functions of teacher development and also about the complexities of dialogue-based professional education within these settings and potentially within the classrooms where participating teachers work.

Personal Experience Narratives

When people meet in social groups, they tell stories. The oral personal experience narrative arises naturally in the conversation of like-minded people. It is a useful and accessible cultural convention we employ to share experience, order our thinking, and present and negotiate personal and social identities (Stahl, 1989). Teachers are no exception, and research finds that when they gather to explore ideas about their role and practice, they liberally fill their conversations with personal experience narratives (Clandinin & Connelly, 1987; Florio-Ruane, 1991).

Our interest in both the psychology of adult learning and sociolinguistics intersects with our interest in personal experience narrative. Jerome Bruner (1986) calls narrative a fundamental mode of thought. The mind's fundamental work, in this view of cultural psychology, is to actively internalize narrative discourse: to compose, retell, and revise our own life story (Clark, 1997; Wertsch, 1991). Like conversation, narrative is a persistent discursive convention that the mind dynamically appropriates to order knowledge and make meaning of experience. Personal experience storytelling is therefore a potent practice for learning.

The conversational personal narrative is also a communicative and expressive form, and has been likened to a kind of verbal art (Abrahams, 1977; Swidler, 1995). As a "way of speaking" (Hymes, 1974), narrative is eminently cultural and rooted in the social life of a group or community. The personal narrative as social practice is used not only for the representation of experience and knowledge. It is also a rhetorical device that group members reflexively employ to negotiate personal and social (group) identities, to persuade each other that what they know, what they do, and who they are—as individuals and as a social unit—are viable and vital.

Educational researchers find that personal narrative is a powerful medium not only for conveying what teachers currently know and believe, but also for exploring new ideas and negotiating difficult experiences and challenging points of view (Harris, 1995; Hollingsworth, 1994). The reconstitution of experience through personal narrative allows for safe exploration of uncharted territory (e.g., teaching in unconventional ways) and for imagining the possible (Greene, 1995). We have analyzed personal narratives for insights into how teachers explain themselves to themselves as well as for evidence of their efforts to learn and forge connections with the experiences of other professionals and new sources of knowledge and experience (e.g., literature, films, cultural and child study). Folkloristics and literary analysis provide tools for examining the narratives we have identifed within inquiry group conversations (Swidler, 1995). We have examined these narratives for what they tell us about the negotiated nature of teacher identity and the ways that conversation among peers provides a context for the shaping and reshaping of that identity by telling one's stories and hearing/reading the stories of others. In researching this aspect of sustained and dialogue-based teacher development, we ask the following questions:

1. How do personal experience narratives arise in teacher development groups?
2. What is the relationship between authentic conversation and personal experience narrative? How are stories used in conversations in the group?
3. What is the nature (themes, structure, and content) of these stories?
4. How do participants' narratives illuminate their existing knowledge and beliefs? Do they provide evidence of participants' learning of new ideas and ways to enact their teaching role?
5. In what ways is narrative implicated in maintaining a group's culture and in negotiating individual and communal identities?

CONTRIBUTIONS TO KNOWLEDGE AND PRACTICE

The overarching aim of this volume is to describe, understand, and theorize about the workings of teacher talk within Professional Development and Inquiry Groups. We offer what we have learned about how conversation-based interaction among teachers contributes to their sustainable professional development and what the limits and complications of this form have been. Our continuing conversational journeys with teachers taught us a great deal about the content and process of learning by adult professionals, the role of personal experience narratives in making sense of experience, and the sociolinguistic dynamics of learning- and change-oriented groups. In the long term, we hope that our work will inspire and enable teachers, teacher educators, and others responsible for teacher learning and development to understand and undertake such conversational journeys of their own.

REFERENCES

Abrahams, R. D. (1977). The most embarrassing thing that ever happened: Conversational stories in a theory of enactment. *Folklore Forum, 10*(3), 9–15.

Argyris, C. (1991, May–June). Teaching smart people how to learn. *Harvard Business Review*, pp. 99–109.

Belenky, M. F., Clinchy, B. McV., Goldberger, N. R., & Tarule, J. M. (1986). *Women's ways of knowing: The development of self, voice, and mind.* New York: Basic Books.

Bilelli, L. (1995, May). *Conversation and storytelling in learning to mentor.* Paper presented to the Conference on Teacher Development, Oranim Teachers College, Tivon, Israel.

Bruner, J. (1986). *Actual minds, possible worlds.* Cambridge, MA: Harvard University Press.

Burbules, N. C. (1993). *Dialogue in teaching: Theory and practice.* New York: Teachers College Press.

Cavazos, L. (1994). *A search for missing voices: A narrative inquiry into the lives of women science teachers.* Unpublished doctoral dissertation, Michigan State University, East Lansing.

Clandinin, D. J., & Connelly, F. M. (1987). Teachers' personal practical knowledge: What counts as "personal" in studies of the personal. *Journal of Curriculum Studies, 19*(6), 487–500.

Clark, C. M. (1995). *Thoughtful teaching.* New York: Teachers College Press.

Clark, C. M. (1997, October). *Teacher professional development: How we help and how we hurt.* Plenary address to the International Study Association on Teacher Thinking, Kiel, Germany.

Darling-Hammond, L. (1994). *The current status of teaching and teacher development in the United States.* Background paper prepared for the National Commission on Teaching and America's Future, Washington, DC.

Edwards, P. A. (1989). Supporting lower SES mothers' attempts to provide scaffolding for book reading. In J. Allen & J. Mason (Eds.), *Risk makers, risk takers, risk breakers: Reducing risk for young literacy learners* (pp. 225–250). Portsmouth, NH: Heinemann.

Featherstone, H., Pfeiffer, L. C., & Smith, S. P. (1993). *Learning in good company: Report on a pilot study* (Research Report 93–2). East Lansing: National Center for Research on Teacher Learning.

Florio-Ruane, S. (1991). Conversation and narrative in collaborative research. In C. Witherell & N. Noddings (Eds.), *Stories lives tell: Narrative and dialogue in education* (pp. 234–256). New York: Teachers College Press.

Florio-Ruane, S., & Clark, C. M. (1993, August). *Authentic conversation: A medium for research on teachers' knowledge and a context for professional development.* Paper presented to the International Study Association on Teacher Thinking, Goteborg, Sweden.

Florio-Ruane, S., & deTar, J. (1995). Conflict and consensus in teacher candidates' discussion of ethnic autobiography. *English Education, 20*(1), 11–39.

Florio-Ruane, S., Raphael, T., Glazier, M., McVee, M., & Wallace, S. (1997). Discovering culture in discussion of autobiographical literature: Transforming the education of literacy teachers. In C. K. Kinzer, K. A. Hinchman, & D. Leu (Eds.), *Inquiries in literacy theory and practice: Forty-sixth Yearbook of the National Reading Conference* (pp. 452–464). Chicago: National Reading Conference.

Greene, M. (1994). Multiculturalism, community and the arts. In A. H. Dyson & C. Genishi (Eds.), *The need for story: Cultural diversity in classroom and community* (pp. 11–27). Urbana, IL: National Council of Teachers of English.

Greene, M. (1995). *Releasing the imagination.* New York: Teachers College Press.

Griffin, G. (1991). Interactive staff development: Using what we know. In A. Lieberman & L. Miller (Eds.), *Staff development in the 90's: New demands, new realities, new perspectives* (pp. 243–260). New York: Teachers College Press.

Harris, D. L. (1995). *Composing a life as a teacher: The role of conversation and community in teachers' formation of their identity as professionals.* Unpublished doctoral dissertation, Michigan State University, East Lansing.

Hollingsworth, S. (1994). *Teacher research and urban literacy education: Lessons and conversations in a feminist key.* New York: Teachers College Press.

Hymes, D. (1974). Ways of speaking. In R. Bauman & J. Sherzer (Eds.), *Explorations in the ethnography of speaking* (pp. 433–452). London: Cambridge University Press.

Kohl, H. (1998). *The discipline of hope: Learning from a lifetime of teaching.* New York: Simon & Schuster.

Lightfoot, S. L. (1983). *The good high school: Portraits of character and culture.* New York: Basic Books.

Little, J. W. (1989). Norms of collegiality and experimentation: Workplace conditions of school success. *Educational Evaluation and Policy Analysis, 11*, 165–179.

Little, J. W. (1993). Teachers' professional development in a climate of educational reform. *Educational Evaluation and Policy Analysis, 15*, 129–151.

Orland, L. (1998). *Learning a new language of teaching.* Unpublished doctoral dissertation, University of Haifa, Haifa, Israel.

Palmer, P. J. (1998). *The courage to teach: Exploring the inner landscape of the teacher's life.* San Francisco: Jossey-Bass.

Pfeiffer, L. C. (1998). *Becoming a reform-oriented teacher.* Unpublished doctoral dissertation, Michigan State University, East Lansing.

Rose, M. (1995). *Possible lives: The promise of public education in America.* Boston: Houghton Mifflin.

Rust, F. O'C. (1997, April). *Professional conversations: New teachers explore teaching through conversation, story and narrative.* Paper presented at the annual meeting of the American Educational Research Association, Chicago.

Schumm, J. S., & Vaughn, S. (1995). General education teaching problem: What can students with learning disabilities expect? *Exceptional Children, 61*(4), 335–352.

Stahl, S. D. (1989). *Literary folkloristics and the personal narrative.* Bloomington: Indiana University Press.

Swidler, S. (1995). *Story in context.* Unpublished doctoral dissertation, Michigan State University, East Lansing.

Wertsch, J. (1991). *Voices of the mind: A sociocultural approach to mediated action.* Cambridge, MA: Harvard University Press.

Zellermayer, M. (1995, August). *Teachers forming a community of learners.* Paper presented to the International Study Association on Teacher Thinking, Brock University, St. Catherines, Ontario.

CHAPTER 2

Translating Themselves: Becoming a Teacher Through Text and Talk

Alison Cook-Sather

TO MAKE SENSE OF the complex challenges of learning to teach and teaching, many teachers and teacher educators evoke metaphors. More than "a device of the poetic imagination and the rhetorical flourish," metaphors govern our everyday thoughts and actions in both conscious and unconscious ways (Lakoff & Johnson, 1980, p. 3). Therefore, choosing a metaphor for learning to teach and teaching is not just a linguistic exercise; it is matter of finding a governing concept that deepens understanding and enlivens practice.

Many of the metaphors evoked by teachers and teacher educators point to predefined roles to be assumed, such as executive, therapist, or liberationist (Fenstermacher & Soltis, 1998), or conductor, coach, or referral agent (Ladson-Billings, 1994). But because learning to teach and teaching are dynamic processes in which to be engaged, not fixed states to be embraced, we need metaphors that capture that vitality.

Sumara and Luce-Kapler (1996) describe learning to teach as a negotiation of the dissonances between preservice teachers' preteaching lives and their lives as experienced teachers. Britzman (1991) argues that "learning to teach—like teaching itself—is always the process of becoming: a time of formation and transformation" (p. 8). In the spirit of these dynamic ways of conceptualizing learning to teach and teaching, I offer a new metaphor.

In this chapter I use the metaphor of translation to describe the process of becoming a teacher within the undergraduate education program I direct. Through participating in a project based in the last course they take prior to student teaching, the preservice teachers in this program translate themselves through two kinds of conversation: a text-based conversation between themselves and me and high school students and a spoken conversation among themselves in the college classroom. Conceptualizing teacher education as translation, we can gain a deeper understanding of the process of learning to teach, and we can better facilitate preservice teachers' preparation.

THE METAPHOR OF TRANSLATION

All meanings of the verb *to translate* refer to changing the condition or form of something. To translate can mean to bear, remove, or change from one place or condition to another. It can mean to make a new version of something by rendering it in one's own or another's language. It also can mean to change the form, expression, or mode of expression of, so as to interpret or make tangible, and thus to carry over from one medium or sphere into another. And to translate can mean to change completely, to transform (*Webster's New International Dictionary*).

We generally think of translation in reference to written texts, based on the second definition above: to make a new version of something by rendering it in one's own or another's language. However, as Constantine (1999) argues, translating a literary text is not simply a matter of finding for the words already written in one language corresponding words in another. Translation is more than transliteration; it is the rearticulation of a complex human experience, and it unfolds through the reciprocity between the translator and the text being translated. A translator is situated in a given historical and social context and has experiences and ways of understanding she has developed over time. To produce an effective translation, she reads or rereads a text with an eye toward re-rendering for another reader in another context the experience the text embodies.

A preservice teacher's translation mirrors this process. Nearing the conclusion of this phase of her formal higher education, a preservice teacher preparing to teach at the secondary level is about to re-enter the familiar/strange context of the high school classroom. She considers the self she is at that point, and she anticipates the context of the high school classroom and the active readers of herself that the high school students will be. With these histories, contexts, and readers in mind, she attempts to re-render herself in ways that will resonate both for her and for students.

A preservice teacher's education embodies the other definitions of translation as well. When she becomes a teacher, a preservice teacher changes her condition. She makes a new version of herself. She makes herself comprehensible to others in a new sphere. She is, if she engages fully in this process, transformed.

This is a challenging and potentially daunting process. When she first re-encounters high school students and schools, a preservice teacher might feel uncertain about how to read and respond to them. Rather than embrace a prescribed role, however, and the interpretive lens such a role would provide, she can try out a variety of interpretations and modes of expression. Some of these attempts may work to capture her meaning and student attention, and some may be flat and ineffective. After a number of attempts at rendering herself, a preservice teacher can begin to develop some confidence, even if the language in which she renders herself sounds strange to her ears. After extensive practice she may come to see that the process of becoming a teacher is an ongoing changing of condition and form.

Essential to this conceptualization of translation is the idea that each new translation, each new version of a text or a self, carries inextricably woven within it all previous versions and readings. No two translations are ever the same, but neither are they ever unconnected to previous translations. Thus, a translation is at once duplication, revision, and recreation, with meaning lost, preserved, and created anew. Furthermore, translation is not a one-time occurrence; it is not a single rendering that fixes and defines the text or the self. Rather, translation as I use it in this discussion is both a responsive and a generative interpretive act, and it is a recursive as well as a progressive process of reading and rendering texts and selves in relationship.

THE SETTING FOR TRANSLATION

The setting for this discussion of learning to teach as translation is the Bryn Mawr/Haverford Education Program, an undergraduate, secondary teacher preparation program. Within the final course preservice teachers take prior to embarking upon student teaching, one of the requirements is participation in a project called Teaching and Learning Together. I designed Teaching and Learning Together in the summer of 1995 in collaboration with Ondrea Reisinger, a high school English teacher. The original purpose of the project was to facilitate a mutually informing dialogue between preservice teachers and high school students prior to the preservice teachers' taking on teaching responsibilities during practice teaching (see Cook-Sather, 2000). Through reflecting on my facilitation of this project over the past 5 years, I came to see it as a forum for translation.

Teaching and Learning Together includes a weekly exchange of letters between the preservice teachers enrolled in Curriculum and Pedagogy and selected students who attend a public high school. This written dialogue is complemented and informed by weekly conversations between the preservice teachers and me in the college classroom and weekly conversations between the high school students and my collaborator at the high school. From 1995–1998, I co-facilitated this project with Ondrea Reisinger, then an English teacher at Springfield High School. In 1998 and 1999, I co-facilitated this project with Jean McWilliams, Assistant Principal at Lower Merion High School.

The high school students who participate in this project range in assigned ability levels from special education through gifted, they represent grade levels from tenth through twelfth, and they claim different racial and cultural identities. Participants are selected upon recommendations of teachers at the high school, and permission for their participation is obtained from their parents and from the school. Within the context of their high school, drawing on their experiences as high school students, and with the support of a school-based educator, the students write letters to the preservice teachers that convey their thoughts and feelings about teaching and learning and that respond to the preservice teachers' evolving pedagogical beliefs and approaches.

The partners in this dialogue, the preservice teachers who are seeking state certification to teach or are planning to teach in private schools, face a different challenge in the exchange. Within the context of the college classroom, but having been high school students previously and now planning to become high school teachers, the preservice teachers write letters to the high school students that attempt to communicate their own evolving ideas and also elicit student perspectives on teaching and learning. Furthermore, the preservice teachers interpret both the students' and their own letters in class discussion and in end-of-the-semester analysis papers. A total of 52 preservice teachers have participated in this dialogue project since its advent in 1995.

I am the final participant in this project. I now work primarily in the college classroom, but I was previously both a high school student and a high school teacher. As teacher, teacher educator, and learner, I offer interpretations of the dialogue between the preservice teachers and their high school partners, and I challenge the preservice teachers to engage in this interpretive work for themselves.

WHAT PROMPTS TRANSLATION:
THE FAMILIAR TRAVERSES THE NEW

A translation "bring[s] home to us as though for the first time things to which we have grown all too familiar" (Constantine, 1999, p. 14). As preservice teachers prepare to return to the classroom, they prepare to re-enter a context with which they believe they are familiar. Indeed, they have spent a large portion of their lives in classrooms, and yet are preparing to re-enter in a different role, one they have observed for many years but have not experienced. When they reapproach the classroom as they assume this new role, a tension is created between what is still familiar and what is new. This tension between the familiar and the strange provides the impetus for translation as I discuss it in this chapter.

What is familiar is a product of experience. For 17 years preservice teachers have lived in and observed classrooms as students. They assume, therefore, that they are fluent in the language of schooling and understand the ways of interacting appropriate to that educational context. Over the course of a lifetime spent in school, preservice teachers have developed deeply ingrained assumptions about and images of students (Brophy & Good, 1974; Bullough & Gitlin, 1995; Weinstein, Madison, & Kuklinski, 1995), and they have derived some "well-worn and commonsensical images of the teacher's work" (Britzman, 1991, p. 3). The assumptions and images many preservice teachers bring to their preparation to teach have much in common because, as hooks (1994) points out, "most of us were taught in classrooms where styles of teaching reflected the notion of a single norm of thought and experience, which we were encouraged to believe was universal" (p. 35).

Although they bring with them a set of images of and assumptions about precollege educational contexts and modes of participation appropriate to them, the 4 years preservice teachers spend in college can contribute to the precollege classroom's becoming a strange place. This alienation is due, in part, to the distance between K–12 classrooms and college teacher-preparation programs; in most models of undergraduate secondary preservice teacher education, conversations about teaching and learning are carried on at a significant remove from the places and people they concern—high school classrooms and high school students. Framed primarily in theoretical terms, conducted almost exclusively in college classrooms, and generally limited to exchanges among preservice teachers and teacher educators, these discussions remain abstract explorations of ideas rather than grounded professional preparation. Within such forums, preservice teachers develop pedagogical beliefs and approaches with little or no input from those they are preparing to teach. This is analogous to attempting to render a translation of a text for a context and audience of which one has outdated, vague, or no understanding and yet, perhaps, that one believes one understands. Like the predefined and fixed roles many metaphors offer teachers, the perspective, understanding, language, and sense of self a preservice teacher brings to her teacher preparation can remain fixed in a place and time in the past that no longer exists.

What is new and strange is not only the context revisited after years of distance but also the necessity of speaking in a new voice and creating a new identity. To learn this new language and something about the context in which it is spoken, preservice teachers need to listen to and talk with high school students. Although a number of critics have noted the absence of student voices and perspectives in conversations about teaching and learning (Connell, 1994; Corbett & Wilson, 1995; Erickson & Shultz, 1992; Jenlink, Kinnucan-Welsch, & Odell, 1996; Nieto, 1994; Phelan, Davidson, & Cao, 1992; Shultz & Cook-Sather, 2001; Weston, 1997), there is little evidence that students have been invited to join those conversations.

Teaching and Learning Together positions high school students in direct dialogue with preservice teachers both to contextualize their preparation to teach and to make a clear statement about the validity and worth of high school students' perspectives on teaching and learning. The amplification of the high school students' voices challenges preservice teachers to attend to the language of a constituency that has values and perspectives that might not, initially, make sense to the preservice teachers. This is a challenge to preservice teachers to translate themselves.

LEARNING TO TEACH AS TRANSLATION: AN OVERVIEW OF THE PROCESS

If learning to teach through Teaching and Learning Together is understood as a process of translation, we can acknowledge that there are key transformative moments in learning to teach (Sikes, Measor, & Woods, 1985). We can acknowledge as well that learning to teach is an ongoing project (Borich, 1995; Britzman, 1991; Sumara & Luce-Kapler, 1996). And we can help preservice teachers experience learning to teach as a continuous and integrated process of self-creation.

The process of translation is ongoing, recursive, and cumulative. Yet there are moments or moves that typify the process at different points during Teaching and Learning Together. The first moment is when preservice teachers must read, interpret, and compose letters in their exchange with their high school student partners. Subsequently, after having been engaged in the translation process for several weeks, the preservice teachers focus less on individual word choice and self-presentation and more on the larger interpretive and expressive project in which they are engaged. Toward the end of the semester, as they reflect on the exchange of letters, the preservice teachers offer integrated analyses of their translations.

Class discussions in Curriculum and Pedagogy, in which the preservice teachers discuss with me and with one another possible strategies for interpretation and expression, help the preservice teachers begin, work through, and reflect on the process of translation. After each weekly exchange of letters, the preservice teachers come back to the Curriculum and Pedagogy Seminar with questions about the gaps, disconnects, and frustrations in understanding, as well as points of connection and communication they have experienced. Both I and the preservice teachers in the class offer advice about how to proceed with the translations.

MAKING INITIAL DECISIONS IN RENDERING AND READING

The initial moment in the process of translation is a first attempt at communication; each preservice teacher must read a letter sent by a high school student and, in turn, render herself in a letter sent back to that high school student. At this moment, preservice teachers tend to have one of two reactions: the inclination and attempt to read and re-read the students as they are embodied in the letters they send and to revise their own letters and themselves to better correspond, or the desire to avoid such attempts.

At these early moments, I aim to convince the preservice teachers that there are many ways to translate themselves. I point to the possible definitions and the possible interpretations and expressions they could attempt, both in terms of the language they are developing and the selves they are becoming. I set up a kind of workshop, and I lead or push the preservice teachers into their translations.

Although they have Teaching and Learning Together as a structured forum within which to re-imagine and construct themselves in their letters, many preservice teachers struggle with what to say, how much of themselves to include, what language to use, and how their letters should look. For instance, one preservice teacher, Leslie, explained, "It took me a long time to decide if I was going to type or handwrite the [first] letter" (field notes, October 5, 1995). Interpreting and responding to the high school students is the complement to this challenge; another preservice teacher, Jessica, explained, "My partner was really formal so I wrote back formally" (field notes, September 17, 1996).

Choices about form and tone are choices about translation. Every decision about the way a text looks and every decision about self-representation affects the reader's experience and interpretation, and the preservice teachers must weigh possible meanings, consider audience and context, and make choices about renderings. Both the preservice teachers' decisions and the high school students' decisions in the brief excerpts above illustrate this fact as well as the dynamic and mutually informing nature of translation in this exchange of letters. Rather than a one-way transformation of a single, fixed text or self, the process is like the exchange of a conversation; there is a back-and-forth quality, a recursiveness as well as a progression of meaning making.

The preservice teachers' readings and compositions have implications for both the immediate interaction with these particular high school students and the kinds of teachers these preservice teachers will become. Some initial decisions made by three preservice teachers, Liz, Leslie, and Emily, point to these implications.

Conversation Between Teacher Educator and Preservice Teacher

An exchange I had with Liz in the Curriculum and Pedagogy Seminar of September 17, 1996 highlights the importance of initial decisions about self-presentation. Upon receiving her first letter from Larry, Liz was struck by his assertive language and self-presentation.

> [My student's letter] was very informal. Really honest. Very negative about things he was negative about and positive about things he's positive about. This one comment was very blunt. A name he called one of his teachers. I wasn't sure how to respond.

Preparing to be a teacher—one of those whom Larry is criticizing—Liz is aware that she must respond appropriately as one aspiring to that relationship with Larry and with other students and with the teachers who will be her colleagues.

Recognizing that this is a defining moment, Liz considers various possibilities for choosing a language and positioning herself in the dialogue with Larry. She and I discuss alternatives, such as leading by example and offering directives. I ask Liz to consider whether the choice about self-presentation she makes now will be the same choice she will make when she is in her own classroom, and I suggest that she can try one rendering and see what happens; if it doesn't work, she can try another.

In this response to Liz, my goal is to make explicit the process in which these preservice teachers are engaged, to reassure them that their questions and uncertainties are valid and can be educative, and to encourage them to consider not only the particular relationship they are developing with their high school student partners but what their choices now suggest about the kind of teachers they want to become. My response also suggests that there need not be a single correct interpretation of and response to any given interaction. Rather, there are multiple possible translations that might work for any given context and audience, and part of what Teaching and Learning Together affords the preservice teachers is the opportunity to try on a variety of selves through composing a range of texts.

Liz decided that the best response would be one "that would lead by example." She explains that she decided that she

> wanted [Larry] to realize that I valued what he wrote about in his last letter, but I wanted to do this by showing that I would take the time to thoroughly answer his question and respond to his comments. In response, I hoped that he would value what I had to say and might begin to explain his thoughts more thoroughly. (Dialogue Analysis, December 1996)

Thus Liz translated herself in the way she hoped Larry would translate himself.

A Conversation Between Two Preservice Teachers

The careful thought and action Liz that demonstrates also characterize an exchange during a class discussion between Leslie and Emily (all quotations are drawn from Curriculum and Pedagogy Seminar, September 19, 1995). Discussing how best to comprehend the first letters they received from their student partners and how to respond to those letters, Leslie explains that she took things her high school partner "had written about in a personal narrative about herself and [tried] to formulate some of those into questions in my letter so that she could directly respond to them." Emily adopted a similar approach, choosing "to make the questions interesting so [my partner] could write a letter back." Emily elaborates that she "tried not to overwhelm [my partner] with questions; I only asked a few questions in the first [letter], and I knew I had to ask them in a way she could respond to." Leslie clarified her understanding of this negotiation—"So almost like reframing it"—and Emily reiterated her approach—"Trying to make it real personal."

These initial attempts at translation are not only about producing appropriate and effective letters; they are also about Leslie's and Emily's striving to compose themselves as particular kinds of teachers. Implicit in their efforts is an understanding of a teacher as one who listens to students, takes what they say and tries to make sense of it, and considers how to present ideas in accessible ways. Although they do not state explicitly in this excerpt that this is their image of a teacher, they do so elsewhere. In her final analysis paper, for instance, Emily writes:

> The interaction between Cynthia and me was teaching me how to listen to a student, to analyze her thoughts, to apply them to the formation of my own teaching persona. . . . The relationship we were building brought my reflections back to my own goals of being an effective teacher and interacting with future students. (Dialogue Analysis, December 1996)

Rather than choose among predefined roles, Emily realizes that she can "listen to a student, analyze her thoughts, [and] apply them to the formation of [her] teaching persona." This process of translating herself releases Emily from pressure to conform to a single, prescribed image of teacher, and it challenges her to embrace this process of conceptualizing and presenting herself as an ongoing project, as central to her goal "of being an effective teacher and interacting with future students."

Implications of Initial Decisions in Rendering and Reading

These excerpts from Liz's, Leslie's, and Emily's spoken and written words highlight the centrality of language as a medium of representation and communication in preparing to teach through Teaching and Learning Together. These preservice teachers have just spent 4 years learning to be successful college students, a process that requires that they "learn to speak as we do, to try on the peculiar ways of knowing, selecting, evaluating, reporting, concluding, and arguing that define the discourse of our community" (Bartholomae, 1988, p. 273). College students must engage in this process before they feel the authority or have the fluency to succeed, since participation in the discourse community of the university is required before the skills to do so are learned (Bartholomae, 1988).

With their nascent fluency in the language of the academy, preservice teachers still recall what it felt like not to be able to find words. Yet they have learned to think and speak the language of theory, and, as Cohn (1990) points out, learning a language "is a transformative rather than an additive process" (p. 50). Learning a new language is not simply a matter of adding new information and vocabulary; rather, it initiates the learner into a mode of thinking about people, power, and relationships. To have succeeded as a student in the academic world is to have joined the privileged realm of the theoretical. Speaking the language of this privileged realm distances preservice teachers from rather than brings them closer to the language that high school students speak.

At this initial moment, when the world of the college and the world of the high school classroom are strikingly juxtaposed, the preservice teachers must translate themselves so as to be comprehensible to high school students. My goal in the early part of the semester is to raise the preservice teachers' awareness of the need for translation, while not making them overly self-conscious. When one is faced with new or seemingly unfamiliar languages, practices, ways of understanding, and ways of being, there is a danger of becoming overly sensitized, self-critical, and even paralyzed. One can quickly move from Liz's initial reaction to Larry's letter—"I wasn't sure how to respond"—to feeling unable to make a choice of interpretation or expression. By highlighting the need for translation, and by encouraging and supporting the preservice teachers as they make initial attempts at translation, I convey to them that I believe that they can, in fact, translate themselves into the teachers they want to be.

DEEPER IN TRANSLATION: COMING THROUGH (IN) THE TEXTS

The initial stages of preparing to teach carry particular challenges—deciding how to position oneself in relation to reader and context, interpreting the texts and selves one encounters, finding words to express oneself in response. As the semester progresses, the preservice teachers assume more and more responsibility for re-interpreting and re-rendering themselves and their letters. The teaching selves the preservice teachers are becoming facilitate their production of more appropriate and effective letters; in turn, the responses those letters produce contribute to the shaping of the teaching selves the preservice teachers are developing.

As the preservice teachers assume more and more responsibility for their translations, I work with them as a collaborator—like a fellow translator verifying and encouraging. Conversations in Curriculum and

Pedagogy shift their focus from how to position and articulate oneself to what that positioning and articulation feel like.

Conversation Between Teacher Educator and Preservice Teacher

With the perspective gained from the experience of several exchanges of letters, the preservice teachers begin to point explicitly to the new language they are using and what that language implies about the selves they are becoming. In a discussion of how her "voice" is changing, Nancy, a preservice teacher, expresses the strangeness of this change:

> One thing I notice is that [my partner will] be asking me questions, and I'll be asking about things like workload or what a good class is like. And then I'll re-read what I've written and I'll think, "I sound like such a geek." It sounds like, "Yeah, it's good to have a teacher that pushes you," and stuff like that. But if I'm out with a friend and we're talking about teaching, we just bitch about it, you know what I mean? And it's just interesting to see that when I'm talking to someone who's younger, that I see as the kind of person I would be teaching, I'm already picking up this mindset that is not my mindset, you know what I mean? You know, it's like, "Courses are a really good way to study things you want to study." And on the one hand I feel that way, but I don't usually articulate it that way. (October 1, 1996)

Nancy recognizes that she is changing not only her language but also her position in relation to an educational context and those within it. I suggest that Nancy is neither falsely taking up a position nor speaking falsely; she believes what she is saying ("on the one hand I feel that way"), but what startles her is how she is saying it ("I don't usually articulate it that way"). Her shift in her sense of herself is reflected in her shift in language, and her appeal to be understood—marked by her repeating, "you know what I mean?"—suggests that she wants her own process of translation to be recognized and legitimated.

In response to Nancy, I suggest that in shifting her perspective she will find herself thinking differently and talking differently. I attempt to reassure her about this change, suggesting that she may not feel quite like her same self because she is becoming another version of that self. I try to convey to Nancy that what she is engaged in is a change from one condition to another, a creation of a new version of herself by rendering that self in another language.

Nancy is not resisting this change of self; she is simply disconcerted by it. Sometimes, however, the preservice teachers who participate in Teaching and Learning Together resist the challenge of translation. At these moments, the other translators in the class strive to help their peers gain perspective and take responsibility for translating themselves.

A CONVERSATION AMONG PRESERVICE TEACHERS

One preservice teacher, Martha, felt that she was getting little out of her participation in Teaching and Learning Together. She was extremely frustrated by the exchange of letters, and about a month into the project she basically threw up her hands in surrender. Her classmates stepped in to try to guide her (all quotations are drawn from Curriculum and Pedagogy Seminar, October 7, 1997). One of her peers, Julia, said to Martha, "I keep thinking about this in the context of, if this were one of your students, and my first reaction is that you can't give up and not write back." Another peer, Jessica, suggested approaching the interaction from a different angle: "Is there maybe a nonconfrontational approach you could try? Like, 'Here's my phone number'?" Matt posed a question to clarify his and Martha's understanding of the tone of the relationship: "She's not antagonistic toward you, right?" and building on this point, Jonathan confirmed the possibility of successful communication: "I think you can send her a message that's very clear without necessarily being angry."

After some more discussion, I restated what Martha's peers had already asserted, emphasizing that with students one cannot quantify and judge their participation. Rather, it is the teacher's responsibility to continue to try to make the relationship with students work.

Inspired by this support, Martha left class early to write to her high school student partner. But it took her until the end of the semester to fully realize that she needed to take responsibility for interpreting her high school partner in a different way and for constructing a different self in interacting with high school students. She wrote:

> In becoming aware of how assumptions I made set the stage for the unfolding relationship between Carol and me, I realized that I was judging her according to my interests and strengths; I was defining intelligence solely in reference to myself. I made the mistake of interpreting her different (from mine) writing style and her level of comfort with written self-expression as lack of intelligence. . . . Now I see that I had abdicated my responsibility in our

conversations and in the relationship as a whole. I had felt uncomfortable . . . and my response was to retreat into my own skeptical perspective. Essentially, my failure to assume responsibility for the early steps of our relationship left her foundering. (Dialogue Analysis, December 1997)

Implications of Coming Through (in) the Texts

In these examples Nancy and Martha illustrate some of the challenges of having to learn a new language and try repeatedly to be understood as they engage in the process of translating themselves. Nancy's perspective suggests that it can feel strange and disorienting, and Martha's suggests that, because of that strangeness and disorientation, one can abdicate one's responsibility as a teacher.

Deeper into the process of translation, these preservice teachers wrestle with some of the same challenges as others who translate themselves from one culture and language into another. Some feel, like Rodriguez (1981), that it is impossible to comfortably straddle two cultures and two languages. In his case, translation from his native Spanish to English resulted in the acquisition of formal English, yet it also resulted in an irreparable loss of connection to his previous self, his native culture, his family, and his first language.

In contrast to Rodriguez, Hoffman (1989) acknowledges the conflicts and tensions she experienced in "her hybridization of voice and self" (Soliday, 1994, p. 519), but she also learned to translate "between the two stories and two vocabularies . . . without being split by the difference" (pp. 269, 274). Although they felt torn and disoriented at first, with the encouragement and support that Nancy and Martha received from their peers and from me, they did not end up being "split by the difference" between their former selves and the selves emerging through their translations.

REVISING AND PROJECTING: REFLECTIVE CONVERSATIONS

By the end of the semester, the preservice teachers have made multiple attempts to compose meaningful and engaging letters and, simultaneously, have made significant progress in the unending process of composing effective teaching selves. Looking back over their 15 weeks of exchanges with their high school student partners, the preservice teachers realize how far they have come in their translations. In their final analysis papers, they gather together the key moments of translation over the course of the letter exchange, and they tell the story the collection of those moments composes. We spend the final class meeting of the Curriculum and Pedagogy Seminar talking about what the preservice teachers have learned through their participation in Teaching and Learning Together.

Learning to Converse with a High School Student

Justina's final analysis of her correspondence with her high school partner, Arthur, reflects how throughout her written exchange with Arthur, Justina struggled with how to discern in his stories implications for teaching practice and how to compose her own theoretically grounded ideas in a language and set of practices accessible to Arthur and other students. She explains:

> When I first undertook the dialogue project with Arthur, a junior from Springfield High School, I expected that I would share ideas about education with a person representing those whom I would eventually be teaching. However, his introductory letter listed the types of music he liked, some career possibilities, his after-school job. He did not mention any specific thoughts about education. By the third week, I realized that Arthur was not terribly interested in educational issues, at least not as I had presented them. (Dialogue Analysis, December 1997)

Because she brought an expectation about the form in which Arthur would share ideas about education, Justina found herself disappointed, thinking that Arthur was not addressing educational issues. Her initial response was to "give up" on what she had hoped to get out of the project: a sophisticated dialogue about how to be a good teacher. So, instead of focusing on issues clearly connected to pedagogy, Justina explained that she "strayed from the texts and issues we were covering in Curriculum and Pedagogy and discussed instead a wide range of topics based primarily on interests or thoughts that seemed pertinent at the time" (Barrett, Dialogue Analysis, December 1997).

As their correspondence continued, Justina found that it was effective to share stories from her own experience as a way to invite Arthur to address important issues. She explains that "it was through examples from my personal life that I asked him about such topics as motivation, block scheduling, career choices, community service, and school policies regarding dress codes" (Barrett, Dialogue Analysis, December 1997). Justina shared the same perspective in one discussion in Curriculum and Pedagogy: "My partner wrote a lot [this week], 'cause he responded to a situation I gave him with my sister. I used that as a way in, saying, 'This happened to my sister. What do you think of this?' And he said, 'Oh, wow, that happened to me too'" (Barrett, Dialogue Analysis, December 1997).

Justina found she could elicit responses from Arthur that "embedded his opinion within situations he had experienced or witnessed." As she put it: "His interests and needs came not through a discussion of Freire's pedagogy, but instead from his own personal experience." Although at first Justina expected Arthur to tell her directly what he liked, how he learned, what worked, and what did not, in a language she was accustomed to at college, upon reflection Justina realized that she needed to co-construct with Arthur a language that integrated his narratives and her theories. In her own words:

> I remained mildly frustrated until I realized that I was expecting [Arthur] to speak in my language. Amid our discussions of student voice and its value, I had neglected to realize that his learning, his method of articulation, was through experience and concrete examples. I had sought to give him voice while failing to hear the sound of his individual words. (Dialogue Analysis, December 1997)

This realization led Justina to recognize that not only did she need to learn to listen differently, she also needed to adjust her discourse practices, although not necessarily her ideas and expectations, when conversing with high school students. She recognized that she would have to be careful of her "tendency to use academic jargon and academic approaches" and to avoid alienating students with an exotic vocabulary. She concludes with these insights:

> Although many students may be capable of thinking abstractly, they may not have practice doing so or be comfortable with it. Therefore, if I come into a classroom assuming they can, I may immediately alienate them. I must instead associate concrete examples with what I am teaching. Arthur offered quite a few insights, drawing on his own experience and projecting accompanying conclusions to global significance. Nonetheless, I failed to recognize them because I viewed them only as narratives of experience. (Dialogue Analysis, December 1997)

Justina's comments suggest that she needs to find a language that bridges and integrates her academic discourse and Arthur's experience-based expressions. The translation must be a mutually informing, ongoing negotiation that leads to the creation of a shared language—a text between people.

Learning to Listen to What a Student Doesn't Say

Although it is more often the case that preservice teachers misread a high school student's use of language and self-presentation as wanting in sophistication and lacking substance, as Justina did, the reverse also can happen: A preservice teacher can misread a student as more sophisticated than he might be. In looking back over his correspondence with his high school partner, Jim, Matt describes just such a misreading.

In a class discussion, Matt explained why he was so impressed with Jim: "[It was like] talking to Holden Caulfield because he was so perceptive and aware of his perceptiveness" (Wildman, December 9, 1997). Matt elaborates:

> I was genuinely amazed to read some of these phrases from the hand of a sixteen year old. This is not to suggest that I underestimate teenagers, but Jim struck me as truly remarkable. While it is not uncommon for a student to be aware of what (s)he is learning, it does indeed seem rare for a student to be aware of his awareness. And this double awareness shaped my conversation with Jim throughout the eleven weeks, and it led me to possibly overestimate Jim's ability to deeply engage himself in his ideas, and, even more importantly, led me to underestimate my role in helping him to further explain his ideas. (Dialogue Analysis, December 1997)

In this instance, Matt mistook Jim's eloquence and his awareness of his own learning process as indicators of a more complex and self-supporting understanding than Jim might in fact have had. In other words, because Jim sounded so sophisticated, Matt assumed that he was more advanced, independent, and fulfilled in his engagement in the dialogue than he in fact might have been. I do not believe that Matt is implying that Jim wasn't sophisticated; rather, as his final comment suggests, Jim's sophistication allowed Matt to avoid focusing on what he must do as a teacher to offer scaffolding to help Jim deepen his ongoing analyses and efforts toward self-expression.

Matt did not discern his possible misreading until the end of the semester, when he looked back over the correspondence. Throughout the semester, the conversation had seemed so fluid. Unlike the gaps or disconnects that Justina and others experienced, Matt explained that throughout the dialogue project it always seemed to him that he and Jim "were on the same page." There was no wrestling with definitions, no disagreement about meaning, no obvious discrepancies in interpretation. There was, apparently, no need for translation.

In retrospect, however, Matt had a different reading. He explains that

> throughout this dialogue project it seemed as if we were always on the same page, but to the extent that a struggle within the dialogue appeared absent, my lack of communication with Jim as to what I wanted him to do put us on very different pages. I am not even sure if Jim was capable of really explaining his responses to the degree I hoped for. His talents, which were so obvious through his writing, hid from me that fact that he was not my peer, but rather a sixteen year old boy who was not going to (or could not) simply answer my questions about why he feels this way or what made him feel this way. He is not a college senior who is used to the difficult task of continuous reflection. (Dialogue Analysis, December 1997)

Matt's analysis adds an interesting dimension to the question of what kinds of translation are necessary. Even though two people can seem to make the same meaning out of the same words, what Matt learned is that understanding surface meanings—decoding or literal comprehension—is not enough. A deeper, more ongoing analysis is necessary to discern the subtle and perhaps not so subtle nuances and complexities of a text and a person. As Constantine (1999) argues about translating poetry, one must consider "the total workings of a text, not just the words" (p. 15).

Implications of Revising and Projecting

Matt and Justina articulate clearly the perspective they gained through reflecting on a semester's worth of producing and responding to letters and trying to discern both the selves of their student partners and their own selves they were creating. In "Translating Self and Difference through Literacy Narratives," Mary Soliday (1994) analyzes "those moments when the self is on the threshold of possible intellectual, social, and emotional development," and she explores literacy narratives as "sites of self-translation where writers can articulate the meanings and the consequences of their passages between language worlds" (p. 511). Soliday (1994) suggests that when the students in her basic writing class are "able to evaluate their experiences from an interpretive perspective, [they] achieve narrative agency by discovering that their experience is, in fact, interpretable" (pp. 511–512).

The written analyses preservice teachers produce at the conclusion of Teaching and Learning Together are similar "sites of self-translation." The final analysis of the exchange of letters offers preservice teachers the opportunity to interpret their ongoing efforts at translating themselves. They, too, find that their experiences are interpretable, and their interpretations prepare them for subsequent readings and translations.

LESSONS LEARNED AND FURTHER CONSIDERATIONS

In looking back over the 5 years during which I have worked with preservice teachers through Teaching and Learning Together, I have found that thinking about learning to teach as translation is useful in a number of ways. It throws into relief the kinds of negotiations in which preservice teachers need to engage to promote their evolving sense of identity and responsibility and their changing conceptualizations of teaching, learning, teachers, and learners. The two modes of conversation upon which Teaching and Learning Together is based—the letter exchanges and the seminar discussions—offer, in conjunction, a powerful model for supporting preservice teachers in the process of translating themselves into teachers.

The Interaction of Text- and Classroom-Based Conversation

The linear and recursive quality of the experience and analysis of the letter exchange, the consistent challenge to maintain and analyze a reciprocal interaction, and the ongoing rendering and re-rendering of the self that participation in Teaching and Learning Together requires, offer a unique and generative way of understanding the process of learning to teach. The deliberate and structured steps in the process of translation make visible the complex experience of preparing to teach. Specifically, the primary medium of exchange (letters) and the distance between interlocutors afford preservice teachers the space and time to experience and understand the transformations of themselves that they effect.

The classroom-based conversation serves as a forum within which preservice teachers can process and deepen their translations. Each group of preservice teachers and I spend 15 weeks analyzing where each participant in the dialogue is coming from, where the gaps in communication and understanding are, what it takes to bridge the gaps, and what selves can be produced through an ongoing process of reading, discussing, revising, and re-rendering texts.

On the last day of class, one preservice teacher, Julia, articulated the effects on her thinking of both the text-based dialogue and the class discussions of it:

> I can imagine that going from last year to next semester without this project in between would have been a big shock and I wouldn't have known how to put theory into practice. This project allowed me to think about the letter every week and I could react in whatever way I wanted to react, I could step back, I wrote an analysis of it—I really got a chance to think through what I did, to think about the process we went through. It got me to think about what I'm doing. (December 9, 1997)

The dynamic and holistic nature of translation as Julia describes it and as I have discussed it in this chapter is particularly relevant to learning to teach. Each week the preservice teachers read and render texts, and as they do they look both backward and forward, making choices about how to read the high school students' texts and how to conceptualize and embody themselves in their own texts. The choices they make and the sense they make of those choices have implications for the preservice teachers in the immediate context of the dialogue project and as teachers-to-be.

Developing Identity Through Translation

Through the exchange of texts, the ongoing oral analysis of them, and the culminating written reflections on them, the preservice teachers both maintain a sense of who they are and forge new identities. Looking back from the final moment of the semester, the preservice teachers see this process of identity formation and what it means. In her dialogue analysis paper, Julia writes about her process of becoming a teacher as "affirming the identity I have created for myself" (de la Torre, December 1997)—an identity that makes connections between her former self and the self she is becoming.

Similarly, Martha describes the translation of herself as "a process of self-examination that I not only want to continue, but will have to continue to be the kind of teacher I want to be" (McClean, Dialogue Analysis Paper, December 1997). This understanding of becoming a teacher is far more complex and flexible than the assuming of a teacher educator-prescribed role for teacher. The sense of integration and commitment to process in the identity Julia and Martha have created for themselves makes the responsibility of becoming and being a teacher clear and personal.

The Responsibility of Translation

One consistent experience Teaching and Learning Together throws into relief is that translation of self is a daunting prospect for some preservice teachers. It is not easy to learn the lesson Martha learned: "that I had abdicated my responsibility in our conversations and in the relationship as a whole" (McClean, Dialogue Analysis, December 1997). But it is essential that preservice teachers recognize their responsibility to understand, communicate with, learn from, and teach their students. They need to remember that they must continually ask themselves the question Matt realized he had not asked enough throughout the dialogue project: "What could I have done?" (Dialogue Analysis, December 1997)—to make students feel safer, more invited to participate, better understood, more engaged.

Through engaging in both the text-based and classroom-based aspects of this project, the preservice teachers learned to move away from a deficit model, in which both they and the high school students fall short of expectations. Instead of looking at high school students' texts as being disappointingly untheoretical, as Justina initially did, the preservice teachers can see those texts as embodiments of distinct discourse practices that it is their responsibility to learn. Not only must the preservice teachers learn to interpret student language, but they must take the responsibility for creating with students a shared language—a language that integrates two worlds and maintains the integrity of both parties.

Understanding the ongoing process of learning to teach as translation allows preservice teachers to maintain their own integrity as knowers and speakers as well as develop a new language. As Justina explains, as she translates herself and her language, she can be both "practitioner in the real world and scholar from the academic world"; she and her fellow preservice teachers must "learn to negotiate both realms" (Barrett, Dialogue Analysis, December 1997). So, as with Julia's assertion that once she commits herself to teaching she cannot "return to my former, disconnected way of thinking," once preservice teachers recognize their responsibility, they must move forward with and into it. If preservice teachers understand learning to teach as a process of translation, they instead can learn to integrate and weave words, worlds, and perspectives.

Translation as an Ongoing Process

Learning to teach is a complex, ongoing, and recursive process—the work of a lifetime. Understanding learning to teach as the work of a lifetime suggests that the translating process must begin right away, prior to student teaching, and it must be a dynamic process that prepares preservice teachers for the kind of interactions, interpretations, and expressions that will be required of them as practitioners. Teaching and Learning Together, designed to create opportunities for dialogue between preservice teachers and high school students, proved to be the catalyst for the translation process. Without the opportunity for such dialogue prior to entering classrooms, preservice teachers run the risk of finding themselves unable to communicate and uncertain about how to position themselves in classrooms. If they do not learn to translate themselves, they run the risk of speaking their own language only and not communicating with students, as too often happens in classrooms.

Accepting that learning to teach is the work of a lifetime means that preservice and practicing teachers need forums for conducting inquiry with students. We need to explore communication and learning with students as critical to teacher preparation and professional development processes. As is argued in *In Our Own Words: Student Perspectives on School* (Shultz & Cook-Sather, 2001), to become better teachers, we need to listen to the perspectives of students.

Although the lifelong task of learning to teach must begin during the preservice phase of teacher preparation, it cannot be completed during that phase. It should begin while preservice teachers have the time, the support structures, and the explicit challenge to develop ways of thinking, speaking, reading, and writing that will serve them well in their classroom practice. But until they are immersed in the culture of the classroom, they can progress only so far in the process of translating themselves. If translation becomes the metaphor they use to understand the ongoing work of becoming a teacher, rather than be daunted by the new and often unanticipated differences that they will encounter in each new group of students and each new educational reform produced by policy makers, they are more likely to embrace these novelties as intriguing variations on an activity in which they have been engaged since they began their preparation to teach.

Teaching/Translation as Vital Activities

Twelve years ago, when I was a high school English teacher, I thought of translation only in terms of literary texts. Undertaking graduate study, teaching in a variety of graduate and undergraduate college contexts, and finally making my way into teacher education, I have developed a more complicated understanding of translation. Now, as a learner, teacher, and teacher educator, I use the idea of translation to understand the process of becoming a teacher—a process through which preservice teachers duplicate, revise, and recreate themselves and their texts, and in the process lose, preserve, and create new meaning.

Constantine (1999) concludes his commentary on translating literary works with this reflection: "Translation, it seems to me, is, like teaching, an intrinsically humane activity" (p. 15). He clarifies that he does not mean that all practitioners, both teachers and translators, are humane. Rather, he suggests, "translating is the practice and the proof of that statement by Terence in the second century BC: 'I am a human being. I count nothing human foreign to me'" (p. 15). This sense of connectedness to other human beings, the willingness to find words and ways of being with people, makes translating and teaching vital activities.

Although embarking on the work of translation is challenging and requires extensive support, the translation process can and should continue throughout a teacher's professional life, so that teaching itself can be understood as a continuously unfolding process of re-rendering complex human experiences. To effect translation, one must be forever open to possible new meanings, not willing to settle or interested in settling for fixed and final definitions and interpretations. Translating oneself into a teacher means analyzing, revising, and re-rendering the self in context after context in ways that both preserve what is vital in the former self and create what is vital to the self one strives to become.

NOTE

One rendering of many, this chapter reflects some initial thoughts about learning to teach as translation of self and texts and is inflected by the invaluable insights of Elliott Shore, Alice Lesnick, Jody Cohen, Jeff Shultz, Paul Grobstein, Chris Clark, Scott Cook-Sather, and Jessye Cohen-Dan.

REFERENCES

Bartholomae, D. (1988). Inventing the university. In E. R. Kintgen, B. K. Kroll, & M. Rose (Eds.), *Perspectives on literacy* (pp. 273–285). Carbondale: Southern Illinois University Press.

Borich, G. D. (1995). *Becoming a teacher: An inquiring dialogue for the beginning teacher*. Washington, DC: The Falmer Press.

Britzman, D. (1991). *Practice makes practice: A critical study of learning to teach*. New York: State University of New York Press.

Brophy, J. E., & Good, T. L. (1974). *Teacher–student relationships: Causes and consequences*. New York: Holt, Rinehart and Winston.

Bullough, R. V., Jr., & Gitlin, A. (1995). *Becoming a student of teaching: Methodologies for exploring self and school context*. New York: Garland.

Cohn, C. (1990). "Clean bombs" and clean language. In *Women, militarism, and war: Essays in history, politics, and social theory* (pp. 33–55). Lanham, MD: Rowman & Littlefield.

Connell, R. W. (1994). Poverty and education. *Harvard Educational Review, 64*(2), 125–149.

Constantine, D. (1999, May 21). Finding the words: Translation and survival of the human. *The Times Literary Supplement*, pp. 14–15.

Cook-Sather, A. (2000). Re(in)forming the conversations: Including high school teachers and students in pre-service teacher education. Unpublished paper, Bryn Mawr College, Bryn Mawr, PA.

Corbett, D., & Wilson, B. (1995). Make a difference with, not for, students: A plea for researchers and reformers. *Educational Researcher, 24*(5), 12–17.

Erickson, F., & Shultz, J. (1992). Students' experience of curriculum. In P. W. Jackson (Ed.), *Handbook of research on curriculum* (pp. 465–485). New York: Macmillan.

Fenstermacher, G. D., & Soltis, J. F. (1998). *Approaches to teaching* (3rd ed.). New York: Teachers College Press.

Hoffman, E. (1989). *Lost in translation: A life in a new language.* New York: Penguin.

hooks, b. (1994). Embracing change: Teaching in a multicultural world. In b. hooks, *Teaching to transgress: Education as the practice of freedom* (pp. 35–44). New York: Routledge.

Jenlink, P. M., Kinnucan-Welsch, K., & Odell, S. J. (1996). Designing professional development learning communities. In D. J. McIntyre & D. M. Byrd (Eds.), *Preparing tomorrow's teachers: The field experience—Teacher Education Yearbook IV* (pp. 63–86). Thousand Oaks, CA: Corwin Press.

Ladson-Billings, G. (1994). *The dreamkeepers: Successful teachers of African American children.* San Francisco: Jossey-Bass.

Lakoff, G., & Johnson, M. (1980). *Metaphors we live by.* Chicago: University of Chicago Press.

Nieto, S. (1994). Lessons from students on creating a chance to dream. *Harvard Educational Review, 64*(4), 392–426.

Phelan, P., Davidson, A. L., & Cao, H. T. (1992). Speaking up: Students' perspectives on school. *Phi Delta Kappan, 73*(9), 695–704.

Rodriguez, R. (1981). *The hunger of memory. The education of Richard Rodriguez: An autobiography.* Boston: D. R. Godine.

Shultz, J., & Cook-Sather, A. (Eds.). (2001). *In our own words: Student perspectives on school.* Lanham, MD: Rowman & Littlefield.

Sikes, P., Measor, L., & Woods, P. (1985). *Teacher careers: Crises and continuities.* London: Falmer Press.

Soliday, M. (1994). Translating self and difference through literacy narratives. *College English, 56*(5), 511–526.

Sumara, D. J., & Luce-Kapler, R. (1996, Winter). (Un)becoming a teacher: Negotiating identities while learning to teach. *Canadian Journal of Education, 21*(1), 65–83.

Webster's new international dictionary (2nd ed.).

Weinstein, R. S., Madison, S. M., & Kuklinski, M. R. (1995). Raising expectations in schooling: Obstacles and opportunities for change. *American Educational Research Journal, 32*(1), 121–159.

Weston, N. (1997, Summer). Distant voices, shared lives: Students creating the global learning community. *Educational Horizons, 75*(4), 165–171.

CHAPTER 3

Resistance as a Catalyst in Teachers' Professional Development

Michal Zellermayer

THIS CHAPTER IS a retrospective analysis of data documented during a professional development program for 18 veteran teachers who wished to become staff developers in the field of writing instruction in Israel. The primary data consist of transcripts of conversations that took place during their professional development meetings. The participants in the conversations were invited to join the university-based professional development program for teaching writing as a process, because they had expressed concern about the teaching of writing in high schools and about the slow progress of their students. The program consisted of 28 weekly full-day meetings. Each meeting was devoted to linking teaching practice with theory and research in writing instruction; designing and practicing writing tasks for high school students; reporting on field experiences in the participants' classrooms; and retrospectively reflecting on the theory, on the writing tasks, and on field experiences. The main topics we dealt with were: writing as a problem-solving process; expert writers' strategies and the procedural facilitation of these strategies; the importance of social interactions during writing (e.g., peer and teacher conferences); constructive response to students' writing and alternative methods of assessment;

and features of the classroom environment that enable teachers to provide students with frequent opportunities for writing and authentic audience response. The purpose of the program was to create a team of staff developers who would introduce a significant change in writing instruction at the high school level. My responsibility was to introduce the participants to recent theory and research on writing and writing instruction, to encourage them to write and share their writing with each other, and to help them to teach writing as a process in their classrooms.

The beginning of the program was very difficult. I was frustrated because the teachers were acting merely as consumers, wanting to get tips from me about what to do in class the following day. In time, I realized that I, like the participants, was a product of the consumer culture, expecting them to receive a packaged body of professional knowledge and to accept a predesigned professional development program (e.g., Daniels & Zemelman, 1985) "for their own good." As I showed more interest in their actual needs and desires, they began to talk about their difficulties and celebrate their successful school experiences. The teachers' accounts were offered spontaneously in the context of their learning activities. One or two teachers would offer to tell about their class experiences, several others would react, and a conversation would develop. During these conversations I usually remained an impartial observer, and did not interfere unless specifically asked to do so.

Today the participants in that and subsequent professional development programs are leaders in the field of writing instruction in Israel. Most of them have introduced change into their own classrooms, mentored other teachers in their own schools, and led writing projects in other schools. Many have kept in close touch with me, reminding me of their initial resistance while providing new examples of resistance from their own programs. Their stories have helped me to understand that teacher resistance is not merely a sign of reluctance to change, but "demonstrations of, or defenses of their empowered relationships to curriculum and curriculum knowledge and their active roles in curriculum innovation and change" (Paris, 1993, p. 125).

RESISTANCE AND AGENCY IN TEACHER DEVELOPMENT

During the 1990s, teacher learning has been conceived of as a constructivist, reframing process (Clift, Houston, & Pugach, 1990; Schön, 1987, 1988, 1991) in which, through concrete experience, collaborative discourse, and self-reflection, teachers' knowledge is transformed into new conceptual models, while links between the old and the new are created. By and large, the constructivist model has been accepted as a basis for democratizing teacher education, and for the design of professional development programs based on communication rather than on direct instruction. However, the democratization of teacher education has not made the relationship between teachers and leaders of professional development programs easier. Recent studies of constructivist professional development projects in writing (Allen, Cary, & Delgado, 1996; Bruner, 1992; Johnston, 1997; Lester & Onore, 1990; Miller, 1990; Paris, 1993; Roemer, 1991; Swanson-Owens, 1986) increasingly depict a paradoxical, self-contradictory process, where the participants both teach and learn, conform and innovate, accept and rebel. In these studies, teacher resistance emerges as the other side of the coin of agency. It becomes clear that if we want teachers to develop as agents of change, we also must make room for their resistance and view it as an opportunity for learning (Giroux, 1988). We need to understand how agency is connected to resistance and how resistance can become a catalyst for change. Research on teachers' professional development can teach us a great deal about the social mechanism through which participants in change projects use conflict and resistance to make a connection between new ideas and older ones and to reframe their social environment.

The research reported here is grounded in four assumptions. First, human development is a dynamic process, in which change is all-embracing rather than an accumulation of new items or a transformation of existing items. Second, developmental change is constructed during significant events consisting of social interaction among the participants, with a recognized beginning, middle, and end. In these events, the rules for social interaction are defined as an integral part of the learning process. Third, there is a direct connection between the quality of the social interaction and the impact of the transformational process (Haroutunian-Gordon, 1991). Fourth, facilitation and resistance are reciprocal parts of the same learning process (Cochran-Smith, 1991; Giroux, 1988; Grumet, 1988; Hargreaves, 1994). This work is particularly influenced by theorists who claim that if we want to understand human development, we should look at processes that occur between people in the public world of their everyday lives, rather than probe inside for personal and private processes taking place deep within each individual (Sampson, 1993). One of these theorists, Rogoff (1995), who frames development as a participatory appropriation process, explains that "the participatory appropriation perspective focuses on events as dynamically changing, with people participating with others in coherent events (where one can examine each person's contributions as they relate to each other, but not define them separately), and development is seen as transformation" (pp. 156–157). Similarly, Watzlawick,

Weakland, and Fish (1974) argue that if we want to understand change, we must look at the pattern of social interaction leading to change. In their examples, the interaction leading to change consists of three moves. It begins with the participants' examination of their shared point of view. Eventually, one participant comments on the way he or she has been looking at the events and interpreting them. The comment causes a break in the framing of the event for the other participants, leaving them a little less defensive than before and more open to the new point of view.

When we study social interaction in teachers' learning events, what should we look at? Frake (1997) explains that when we look at talk, we find that people do not so much ask and answer inquiries; they propose, defend, and negotiate interpretations of what is happening. We therefore should study the ways that the participants negotiate their interpretations not only of what is being talked about, but also of what is going on among them. Like Rogoff and Watzlawick and his colleagues, Frake views the participants in constructivist conversations not just as questioners, but also as interpreters of their lives. A conversation for Frake is a social event that "exemplifies a conceptual unit whereby we organize our strips of experience in formulating accounts of what is happening, our memories of what has happened and our predictions and plans for what will happen." These events, he argues, are "proposed interpretations of what is happening at some time and place" (p. 37).

Wertsch (1985), a Vygotskian theorist studying children's early development, demonstrates that there is a lot to be learned about participatory appropriation from social events occurring during mother–child interaction. He found that two things happen during such events. One is risk taking by the child; the other is reflection of this risk taking by the mother. For Wertsch, risk taking and reflection are cognitive tools that mediate the participants' reinterpretation of their own lives, leading to development. Bearing in mind Wertsch's finding, it is interesting to note that Giddens (1991), a critical sociologist studying problems of self-identity in the age of high modernity, goes so far as to single out risk taking and reflection as the two most typical elements structuring modern self-identity. Giddens claims that "modernity is a risk culture. . . . Under conditions of modernity, the future is continually drawn into the present by means of the reflexive organization of knowledge environments" (p. 3).

What is risk taking? Vygotskian learning theorists who tie risk taking to learners' control of their learning process (Pollard, 1993) have shown that risk taking can operate in subtle ways, even in relatively nonrisky situations. In fact, risk is a subjective, context-dependent feature of social events. Furthermore, it is the social events in which the participants take risks that are considered by them as critical and significant. If risk taking is subjective, how then can it be assessed? Frake (1997) proposes that significant social events usually are considered by the participants as reportable occurrences, to fill in conversations, letters, diaries, and field notes, and that researchers can assess them through such reports.

However, we still have to understand how the need for risk taking and for "revolutionary" acting against the grain is aroused, what motivates it, and how agency is tied to resistance. An important step in this direction has been made by feminists who position learning as a process involving the construction of subjectivity as a paradox of conformity and resistance. Within this new view of learning, Mahoney and Yngvesson (1992) present learners as active subjects who participate in the construction of the wants and needs that culture enjoins them to desire or resist. These authors describe the creative experience of the self as tied to two contradictory desires: to connect to authority and to resist it. Mahoney and Yngvesson (1992) propose that

> only by connecting desire with agency can we explain the reproduction and transformation of social meanings as other than unintended consequences of action and provide a theory of an agentic subject who is neither intentional nor driven by "need deficit." (p. 45)

Like the Vygotskian theorists, Mahoney and Yngvesson turn to studies of early childhood development for examples that support their theory. They show that agency is tied to a power struggle in which the infant, on becoming aware of the possibility of being both connected and autonomous, experiments with the extent to which he or she has control over the caregiver. In addition, they draw on historical accounts of nations, illustrating that the very dynamics of unequal power relations and contradiction evoke creativity and change. Mahoney and Yngvesson's important contribution is in proposing that risk taking, creativity, and acting against the grain must be understood in the context not only of acting and speaking but also of reacting and listening. It is the interplay of the two that shapes "the subjective forms of desire, empowering subjects who are not only complicit but capable as well of resisting relations of domination" (p. 71).

The text that follows provides examples of teachers' need to connect and to resist, and shows how conversation became a space for these teachers to transform this need into agency.

FOUR TRANSFORMATIONAL EVENTS

In this study, I participated as researcher, in addition to my position as teacher educator. Data for the study included transcribed audio tapes of the teachers' unsolicited conversations in the program, field notes of these meetings taken by two graduate students who assisted as participant observers, and the teachers' learning logs that I read and responded to regularly. The analysis consisted of identifying significant events in the teachers' conversations that brought about transformation, in contrast to the more gradual accumulation of learning that took place in the program, and then isolating a particular structure of social interaction that was common to all of these events. The identification of the excerpts to be analyzed was based on the participants' oral and written responses to the professional development program. The validation of these reports was achieved through the convergence of the three sources of data mentioned above, representing three different perceptions of the same events—those of the participants, of the observers, and of myself, the teacher educator—and through the layering of data across time. The analysis of these excerpts was done through a dialectical comparison between the data and theory, yielding a structural unit for describing the social interaction as well as focal themes.

The structural analysis of the excerpts illustrated that, for these teachers, conversation leading to learning typically consisted of three moves. While the teachers reacted to the tasks from the point of view of their old attitudes and knowledge, one of them volunteered to share a specific teaching experience with the group. Through her account, she exposed her own problems and difficulties, providing evidence that some of these teachers' claims might not fit her new experience. Her unsolicited self-exposure often was followed by expressions of surprise from others in the group. But more important, it triggered a reflective reassessment of the risk taker's experience and of the views expressed by the other participants in the discussion. These two turns of exposure and risk taking followed by reflective assessment formed a three-step structure taken by two significant participants: the risk taker and the reflective assessor, with the intermediary support of the other participants, as illustrated in Figure 3.1.

Step 1:	Step 2:	Step 3:
A "risk taker" exposes herself and shares an unsolicited account of her teaching experience.	The group or a member challenges the account.	The "reflective assessor" decontextualizes the account and generalizes about it.

Figure 3.1. The three-step pattern of teachers' reframing of events.

In what follows I present four exemplary excerpts from events occurring at different phases of these teachers' learning. I describe the particular social structure of each of the events and illustrate how, by means of this structure, the teachers confronted and reframed their old notions about writing instruction and about students' learning, and how, while doing so, they clarified and enhanced the structure of the events. I show how the teachers' willingness to take risks was tied to their resistance and their connectivity, as the focus of these forces shifted from one event to another.

Event 1: The Reframing Structure Emerges

During the first two sessions of the program, it was clear that the participants saw themselves as victims of their teaching situation: They blamed the students for their difficulties, saying that "the students have no general knowledge," or "they have nothing to write about." At the same time, they resisted my demand for their active participation in the program and expressed anger that I did not provide ready-to-use ideas for classroom teaching. They were especially uncomfortable with the school-like reading and writing activities they were pressed to take part in. One of them voiced the general feeling of the group at that time toward these activities: "We feel coerced. This is no longer a part of our lives." There was a general feeling of uneasiness about sharing their writing with the group. One teacher said: "To expose myself in front of people I don't know . . . is too difficult." And another: "I feel terrible. I want to jump in and get it over with."

In preparation for the third meeting, they were asked to observe their own classrooms and take notes on the ways in which their students dealt with writing assignments. This, they felt, was an appropriate task. Several participants even volunteered to share their findings with the group. Sarah, one of the veteran teachers, opened the discussion by saying: "I wanted to take advantage of the task for this program, and presented it to my class as a writing assignment. I gave them a list of questions about their own writing, and said: 'I have a problem. I have a task for a class. I need your help.' I told them that they did not have to write their names, and could include criticism of the writing classes. . . . I managed to persuade them to write. I have a number of unexpected responses here." She read aloud a text written by a student who, she said, "is intelligent but has problems in academic writing." It was the student's account of her own difficulties in writing for school as distinct from writing outside of school. Although, according to Sarah, this student's written performance was generally very poor, she managed to describe her own writing process in a coherent and engaging way. The discrepancy between the student's performance in general and for this specific task became the main topic of the teachers' conversation. Sarah explains:

> I really don't know where to start. There were many interesting texts. For example, this girl. Hers is an exceptional story, because I think she is very intelligent. She expresses herself very well orally, but her writing is very poor; you cannot get a thing out of her. I asked the science teacher, and she said the same thing: "I cannot follow what this girl writes, yet I feel that she understands my lessons." The girl is very pleasant and her expression is friendly. She projects communication and sympathy, and I could never understand her problem in writing.

Sarah reads the student's paper:

> This year the writing classes are more helpful than before. Yet I feel I cannot get the best out of them in the pressured condition of writing in class. The teacher's explanations help me in a general way, but I would have liked them to focus on my particular problem. I find it difficult to impress others with my writing. I do not know how to translate my thoughts and the flashes of my ideas into words and paragraphs. Apparently, the particular form the composition has to take, the order, the precision—these cause my problem in writing—this need to fit things into a frame, to put x before y so as to get a high grade puts pressure on my school writing.
>
> I like to write with a pen, because it feels like painting. I like to write in a green quiet environment. . . . I don't like to write about predefined topics. It is easier to write about things that are seemingly unrelated.
>
> At school I pick the topic I know most about, or have definite opinions on. I also prefer topics that are close to my heart. At first, I make a list of whatever I know. The problem starts when I have to transform the list into paragraphs. The greatest difficulties arise when I have no ideas and ways to find solutions.

Two teachers react to what Sarah has read:

EDNA: She is a skilled writer.
SIMA: She is not a skilled writer. Her awareness has been sensitized.
EDNA: Her self-criticism is harsher than our criticism.

From a theoretical point of view, two important issues were implicitly raised here by the teachers: the relationship between reflection and writing ability, and the focus on students' ability rather than on students' deficiency. At this point, Sarah and Edna were the only ones who showed intuitive awareness of these issues. Sarah explained how she had become aware of the other frame: The written response was a deviance from the student's normal behavior; it made her realize that this student's performance varies in different contexts; as a result she now doubted her own understanding of the student's situation. The other teachers, however, perceived the deviance as an artificial and meaningless response to the fact that the student's sensitivity had been heightened. Edna seemed to be the only one who appreciated the significance of self-awareness. The other teachers were not yet able to see the significance of students' self-reflection in learning to compose.

Two significant protagonists can be identified: the risk taker (Sarah) and the reflective assessor (Edna). Clearly, this was a risk-taking episode for Sarah. She had presented herself in a new way to her students, revealing to them that she was participating in a professional program and needed their help for a task assigned in that program. She also took the risk of exposing herself and her classroom experience to the program participants. She was the first to bring classroom data as evidence of a difficulty she was having, for which she needed help. In response to the risk-taking move, Edna came up with a reflective assessment of this part of the event: "The student's self-criticism is harsher than our criticism." This assessment alluded to the teachers' initial difficulties in describing their own writing processes. It was as if she said: "This poor writer has done a better job of describing her own writing process than we have, and this may indicate that the problem is ours, rather than hers." Her statement had a strong potential for turning the teachers' resistance into connecting with the students' experience. She reframed Sarah's account of her direct teaching experience, making it a trigger for introspection. This was an important opportunity for the teachers to reflect upon their "blame the student" attitude. However, no one did. Apparently the teachers were not yet ready to make use of this opportunity and reflect on their own situation. The next part of the conversation demonstrated that the teachers avoided a discussion of their own difficulties, as had been suggested by Sarah and Edna, and focused instead on the difficulties the student described in her own writing process:

RAYA: She has a problem with her audience. She does not know what to select from her knowledge and how to organize it for her teacher. This is a problem of confidence. I would strengthen her confidence in what she knows and show her how to adjust it to her audience. . . .

SARAH: I am glad you said that, because I did go to her and tell her that her writing was wonderful, and asked her to write me more. . . .

SIMA: I don't understand what you are talking about. I see her problem differently. She has an organization problem. She does not know how to organize her ideas, and this is a problem that many other students have. As a result, they develop a negative attitude toward the writing task.

RAYA: You have to consider that even in biology, where she knows the subject, she has difficulty writing. Why is it hard to organize her writing in biology and yet it was not hard in this writing task where she had to describe feelings? She must have problems with intellectual things.

SARAH: This topic was right for her.

NAOMI: That means that one of the instruments we could give her is . . .

RUTH (interrupts): A plan.

RAYA: In biology she gets a plan.

At this point, the teachers still viewed the student's "deficiencies" as a separate topic of discussion unrelated to their own learning process. As a result, they were still unable to reflect on the event and perceive any implications for their writing instruction. For a while, it seemed that Sarah would make another effort to push the discussion in the direction of the student's perspective on her own difficulties and needs. Sarah insisted that the topic was right for the student. Ignoring this claim, Ruth suggested that the student needed a plan. Sarah then could have pushed this idea further by saying that the student needed additional opportunities to write about topics that were right for her, but she did not. Instead, Sarah regressed from risk taking into self-defense:

I have a problem. I understand that this student has a difficulty but I do not have the tools to identify it, to focus on it. How should I define her problem when the definition may be psychological and unrelated to what she has written here?

Although these teachers were experienced in problem fixing, they were less experienced in problem setting. As a result, they discussed a student's "deficiency" without making a serious attempt to define the problem for the discussion. Without clarifying the source of this student's difficulty, or their own difficulty in identifying it, they offered solutions to her "problem." This part of the conversation was not constructive. The participants seemed to compete in coming up with the best cure, without allowing each other to complete one thought or to fully elaborate on a solution. They never really used the discussion to construct and juxtapose different descriptions of the same phenomenon. This supports the claim made by Burbules and Rice (1991) that without collaborative conversation there is a heightened feeling of one's own deficiency and the deficiency of others, which manifests itself in seeking to blame others for one's subjective feeling of incompetence.

One may question whether this episode, which did not achieve critical inquiry, was a significant event at all. In my view, the event had learning potential because an alternative professional model began to emerge. Although the teachers did not face the new model consciously, or make any serious attempt to compare what the two kinds of professionalism offered, the pattern of the learning event itself was created. Within the pattern described in Figure 3.1, the teachers discovered the relevance of the event to the two contexts of action—the professional development program and the school. This new way of looking at their own activity enabled them to repeat and refine the acts of risk taking and reflective assessment. The following examples of these teachers' learning events show that through this three-step structure the two contexts of action eventually connected and defined the teachers' zone of proximal development (Vygotsky, 1978). Within this zone, the classroom tasks suggested by the program helped them discover their students' perspective and potential—and in time they also would learn that a student's response was relevant to their own development. In a spontaneous conversation with several teachers after this meeting, one of them said to the participant observer: "I seriously considered dropping out of this program because I did not see its relevance to my needs, but today, after I read my students' responses, I have decided to stay."

Another important contribution of this event was that it allowed us to locate the focus of the participants' resistance at the beginning of the program and follow its shifts during subsequent events. At this early point the teachers still resisted the program and the tasks they were given, but demonstrated a need to connect to their students and to make meaning of the students' responses to them. Their motivation for risk taking was tied to understanding that the program tasks created opportunities for them to discuss their students' ways of responding to them.

Event 2: Problem Posing

The second event I focus on took place in the eighth meeting of the program, at a critical stage when, for the first time, teachers confronted their own assumptions about control and ownership of school-based learning and began to see issues from a different point of view. The crisis can perhaps be best understood through a detailed description of the teachers' confrontation with a visitor (Yael), who described how she taught writing. Yael said she used no textbooks, but directed her students' learning through correspondence in dialogue journals. Yael talked enthusiastically about her students' ownership of their own writing, but several members of the group had strong reservations about her way of teaching because they felt it lacked structure and control:

> SARAH: I have a problem. I don't mean to criticize you, but I am concerned about what you did not do. What about the need to teach them responsible structured writing?
>
> RUTH: You do it [journal writing] for a whole year! If you do it in seventh grade, you're not going to do it in the eighth!
>
> YAEL: There's no end to this source. It's a source of life.
>
> RUTH: Are you going to do it in the tenth? And eleventh? They need to write a composition about some topic.
>
> YAEL: They learn to write. There's no need to teach them. They learn by writing.
>
> DINA: What happens when they reach twelfth grade? What happens when there is a matriculation exam? Your students at the end of ninth grade may be better writers, but you don't deal with certain skills at all.
>
> YAEL: Why not?
>
> DINA: The question is not whether you enjoy it or whether the student enjoys it. It's a question of responsibility. Do you feel that your students, after corresponding with you for 3 years in a dialogue journal, are prepared for a matriculation exam the next year? The exam has its own criteria.

Yael explains that in the journal students write about a wide range of topics that they themselves initiate, such as personal problems, pets, interpersonal relationships, and learning problems, as well as writing problems. Sarah, however, insists that what Yael does overlaps with the counselor's job. In response, Yael tells about a student who claimed to have nothing to write about. She says she suggested that he write about a dream.

> EDNA: Why did you choose that?
> YAEL: Because I felt like it.
> EDNA: But as a teacher, you should never say "Because I felt like it."
> YAEL: What is wrong with that?
> EDNA: It is all right. I did not say it wasn't. Yet, it seems that things should be more controlled.
> TOBY (in an attempt to find a solution): You are telling about your experience with seventh, eighth, and ninth graders. If we do it in the twelfth, I suppose that more mature topics will come up. They [the students] will write and we will respond and while doing it we'll show them how to elaborate, all by way of correspondence. We are still captives of our own misconceptions—if we try it, I'm sure we'll succeed.
> RUTH (picks up from there): I envy your students and you. With my students, I write comments on their compositions; they get their writing back, look at the grade, and throw it away. I say: "What about all the hours of work I've invested?" They don't even look at it. Your students read the comments and learn. I think it's incredible. It's really exciting.
> EDNA (takes another turn in the discussion and tells of her experience in dialogue journal writing with her students): We need to experience a metamorphosis. I have to tell you what happened yesterday. Can you believe that my students said to me: "Teacher, you're disturbing our writing." I said: "Excuse me, I'll keep quiet." Seriously, I'm telling you. This happened to me yesterday for the first time. It happened because they wrote to me. I enjoyed it. They talked to me.

The tension between teacher control and student ownership is central to the teaching of writing. The teachers were familiar with this tension in theory, but could not conceptualize its practical implications. Their problem came to light when the visitor spoke about the significance of the teacher acting as an authentic audience for students' writing. The teachers brought up the limitations imposed on their teaching by the matriculation exams, as if trying to say: "How can we encourage students' ownership of their learning when we are not owners of our own teaching?" They did not ask themselves why they felt that the two demands (to serve as an audience and to prepare students for matriculations) were mutually exclusive. When Yael insisted that the two demands could be met simultaneously, the difference between her conception of teaching and theirs became even more pronounced.

On the basis of their experiences in the program as well as with theoretical papers on responding to students' writing (e.g., Atwell, 1987), several of the teachers had already tried some informal corresponding with their students. Their experience indicated that their students responded well to the visitor's way of teaching. They understood that keeping dialogue journals was not the main issue. They knew that they were actually talking about being able to release control of their students' learning. Yet it was still difficult for them to conceptualize what such ownership meant in terms of their students' learning, their own teaching orientation, and the curriculum. In order to be able to do this, they admitted that they needed to experience a metamorphosis.

They evidently had reached an understanding that they had to reframe their point of view in order to experience a real change. They themselves suggested the different points of view to replace their own: that of the learners and that of the teachers' personal satisfaction. But at this point these options were still distant and abstract. They had not yet formed a theory of action.

A closer look at the structure of this event showed that the typical three-step pattern of the teachers' learning events appeared when the group condemned the visitor's way of writing instruction as not "controlled" enough, and a risk taker (Ruth) told the visitor that she envied her students. This shift to the students' perspective triggered the reflective assessor (Edna) to turn the focus toward introspection, generalizing about the situation: "We need to experience a metamorphosis."

Clearly, the group's discussion and especially the comment by Toby ("We are still captives of our own misconceptions") facilitated the intervention of the risk taker. The reframing process began when Toby's comment caused a break in the framing of the event for the other participants, leaving them a little less defensive and more open to the new point of view. It culminated when the reflective assessor (Edna), who formerly had expressed conflict with Yael, made her reflexive comment expressing the need for change.

They were now able to elaborate on the two different world views and explain the differences between them. They experienced the two worlds as raising conflicts that they were not yet able or willing to resolve. These were conflicts between the new values they were in the process of discovering and the values of the system to which they belonged. While holding on to their old views, however, they started to explore the new view. They already knew that in order to incorporate this view into their own lives, they would have to abandon principles of control that governed their teaching. But they were not yet ready to make this commitment.

This event was a step forward for these teachers in the way they structured the event and in the capacities they displayed for critical inquiry. In contrast to the first event, they explicitly posed a problem and discussed its implications. The focus of the interaction became an object of reflection in its own right. The question asked by Yael: "What is wrong with responding to students the way you feel?" was fully contextualized. It was taken from the teachers' own claims, and the teachers reacted by making a serious attempt to confront it. Although not yet ready to work toward a solution to this problem, for the first time the teachers treated the problem as their own, rather than their students'. They were aware of what their problem was and of what they would have to do in order to solve it.

In this event I see progress in the teachers' reframing process, and also a shift in the focus of their resistance and connecting. The teachers' resistance is no longer directed toward the program and toward me. In this episode, Yael, a visitor, was the focus of their resistance. In the beginning, they seemed to be united against her. But their ability to connect with her students and empathize with the teacher helped the group to take the first step toward the position that Yael represented and channel their resistance toward agency.

Event 3: Generalizing the Context of the Problem

A third example comes from a transcript of a session devoted to developing procedures for holistic evaluation of students' compositions. By the twelfth meeting, the teachers had become more familiar with the theory of teaching writing as a process—particularly its emphasis on formative holistic evaluation (Cooper, 1977) and on responding to students within their level of development. On the basis of this theory, Susan was the first to construct a new approach to writing assessment, in which an evaluation scale was constructed for each class at each phase of its development. She was now confident she could trust her own judgment and reject the standardized (nondevelopmental) formats for evaluation. While she advocated a context-dependent approach to assessment, the other participants still held on to their old objectivist view. They were unable to extend ideas about formative evaluation to writing assessment. Above all, they could not accept that the assessment of student learning is a subjective process, in which acceptance of conflict and ambivalence is an integral part.

This inhibition was significant to their development. It underscored their need to develop an awareness of their own biases as well as of the nature of subjectivity in general. The discussion gave the participants opportunity to do both. The following excerpt from their conversation illustrates how they realized that teachers, like other practitioners, had to face their own subjectivity and act according to their understanding of what this meant for them and for their students:

> SUSAN (referring to an example of unsatisfactory writing): I asked the students for a personal impression, but this one is very short, undeveloped, and unconvincing.
> SARAH: What is "convincing"? That's not a criterion. It is a very subjective thing. This is a way of legitimizing prejudice. I am looking for an evaluation procedure that will not depend on subjective criteria.
> JUDITH: Exactly. This is the problem.
> DALIA: The example we had here may be esoteric. We need an evaluation scale that will stand by itself.
> SUSAN (defending the examples of students' writing she brought to the program): In my class there are a number of students who write like this. At least three or four.
> SARAH: Why do you think that the model [for the ideal text] must come from the class, and that we should not use an objective model for all of our students? This annoys me. I feel that this problem exists only in writing instruction.
> SUSAN: Because we have better and worse classes. We must work with what we have. There should not be a situation where no one in the class can reach an A.
> RAYA: We face problems of subjective evaluation in all areas of life.

This event was similar in structure to the former ones. It began when one teacher (Susan) volunteered to provide examples of her students' texts. Again it was the participant presenting the data who took the role of the risk taker. Her examples generated a group discussion about her "subjective" evaluation. But she persisted in defending her belief in con- textualized, performance-based evaluation, with some additional data from her students. Her self-exposure was immediately challenged by Sarah. But the challenge only encouraged Susan to continue her own line of thought.

The turning point occurred when Raya, the reflective assessor, pointed out that subjective decision making takes place in all areas of life. This was the first time that these teachers had viewed themselves as professionals engaged in a problem-solving process where the problems were not specific to the teaching of writing or even to teaching at all. This re-contextualization of the teachers' experience, presenting it in a generalized manner and a broader context, was an important step in reconstructing their expectations of themselves and their environment and in redirecting their attention from external factors to themselves. They needed to step outside the boundaries they had set around their own problem-solving context in order to be able to re-examine their own problem-solving abilities.

In this event, for the first time, the teachers attempted to use concepts of the new constructivist view of teaching writing in their own frame of reference. Hitherto, they measured student writing against the values of the traditional system in which they were working. Their inability to deal with the conflict was related to their perception that the problems that came up in the discussions were confined to the area of writing instruction. They now learned that there could be multiple perspectives on a problem, such as the evaluation of students' writing, and that conflicts arising from these multiple perspectives can be resolved by reframing the context of the situation. In this event, for the first time, a problem was posed by the group members themselves. They evaluated the problem in terms of their own experience and on the basis of more general knowledge. As a result of that evaluation, they were able to reframe their old notions and reach a conclusion that allowed for a solution to the problem.

Event 4: Looking Inward

The fourth event was initiated by an unplanned visit by the superintendent of language teaching to our twenty-first meeting. Raya volunteered to present the program to the visitor. She started by describing her school, which she said represented the entire population of the country, and then switched to the history of her professional career:

> The topic of composition writing, of oral and written expression, has always been tied to that of comprehension, and there has always been frustration in that area. There was a feeling of vagueness, that we did not know what to teach. We kept going to inservice programs and taught according to what we saw there, but the results were not satisfactory. The students did not progress, and that showed in their matriculation exams. With low-level students, there was a feeling of complete despair; we felt there was nothing we could do to change this. I myself have been a teacher for 32

years. I felt burnt out. Six months ago I applied for early retire-
ment because of the feeling that my work made no difference. I
had initially started working with such idealism, such enthusiasm,
I invested so much energy. . . . Then I was offered the opportunity
to join this program and I started, like everybody else, with a feeling of doubt, hesitation, and great anxiety. Then something very interesting happened. First of all, my attitude toward my students
changed. My attitude that, I admit now, bordered on disrespect,
changed so dramatically. I realized that I was dealing with people
who could learn much more than they had ever done. I have proof
that children who had never written, who were afraid to write because of their mistakes, were starting to write, to become interested in writing. I discovered that I was not only affecting their
writing abilities but also their thought processes, their view of the
world, and their self-respect. I now blame myself for my lack of
success. I have reconsidered my decision to retire.

Naomi took off from that point:

There are two issues in writing instruction: There's the awareness
of the writer. We have to help them reach this awareness. This cannot be done by saying to them: "In every composition there is a beginning, a middle, and an end, and there are different types of beginnings." This will not work at all because the student is focused
on the problems of "Where am I going? Who is my audience?" etc.
But an additional sort of awareness is that of the teacher. There is
a change in teachers' awareness. We came here to get recipes. We
got a complete change. And this is actually our duty outside this
program. Just as we are enthusiastic to do it, we could pass this enthusiasm on to other teachers.

Toby added:

In my school, as in many other schools in the A and B tracks, students are underachievers in writing development. Because it is impossible to work with all the students, it is important to start with
teachers. At this point I would like to stress that in order to facilitate teachers' learning, the teacher educator must project that he or
she too has changed and that this change was so meaningful that
it could affect other teachers as well. Otherwise, they cannot be
trusted. In this program I have become . . . it is difficult to say . . . I
have become a prophet. "A composition prophet," I call myself

sometimes. I don't want to use superlatives that will seem exaggerated, but I feel that I am in the midst of a great awakening. On the other hand, I am alone, and there is nobody to help me. . . . The students now prefer writing classes to literature classes. They can't wait for their journals. They beg me for them. I want to stop, I am tired. I read these journals till 2 or 3 o'clock in the morning. It's exciting. Before, when I gave them a topic for a composition they used to say: "We have nothing to write about." Now they sit for 3 hours and write. When I taught them a few revision strategies, they suddenly asked: "Why didn't we start doing this in first grade?"

This fourth discourse event also was initiated by the risk taker, who opened it with a reference to students' perspectives contextualized in her own personal experience. Her account was assessed by two reflective assessors: one generalized the risk taker's personal experience to two issues in writing instruction—the awareness of the student and that of the teacher, and the interaction between them; the other speaker generalized the experience to the interaction between a teacher's change and that of students or other teachers. As yet another illustration of the three-step pattern, this event demonstrates the significance of interacting with students, with students' writing, and with the development of other teachers in the school. The teachers used the three-step pattern to describe their own zone of proximal development; they reflected on significant interactions at school with their students and colleagues, and in the program with the other participants and the reading and writing tasks. Taking place in an advanced phase of the teachers' developmental journey, this event was an example of the reflexive effect of learning. In addition to learning about their students' learning and about the effects their instruction had on students, the teachers learned about their own learning process and how to revise it.

The teachers' discourse was suffused with new language demonstrating their induction into another way of life. They now spoke about the holistic, dynamic character of literacy. Teaching writing became a positive humanistic enterprise that focused on the whole child as well as on their own self-identity and self-transformation. When the teachers began to focus on their own change process, they talked about their own difficulties instead of those of their students. They reflected on their initial resistance and on their own need to connect to their students, and this created in them the sense of agency for themselves, for their students, and for their colleagues. It became apparent that they had not only reframed their initial view of learning and teaching, but also managed to coherently integrate the professional development program into their professional autobiographies. In a narrative style they told the superintendent how they now held a different view of themselves, of others, and of the situation, and realized that their difficulties could not be attributed solely to external factors. Rather than blaming the students for their own failure, they now perceived students as catalysts for their own change. Not only did they demonstrate an understanding of the impact of their feedback on students, but they identified their students' responses as the major influence on their change: The teachers' risk taking had been rewarded by their students' enthusiastic response. They had given up the "deficiency" view of students' learning and consequently were able to shift their focus from their students' "problems" to their own and to engage in a process of inquiry about their own practice. Students' responses were now their measure of whether their application of the new theory was correct and of whether they should try other theoretical constructs of the new view of teaching.

Now that they had changed, the teachers wanted to become change agents for other teachers. No longer did they look outward for a curriculum or a set of materials to bring about that change; they looked inward at their own change in order to help them promote change in others. They made the connection between change and the ability to reflect on action. They understood the relationships between self-awareness and change for the student as well as for the teacher. They clearly had adopted a different frame for their own practice, which made them more aware of the change process itself. Most important, they had become aware of the difference between first-order change, in which they were changed but the system was not, and second-order change, in which the system also was affected. Because they had undergone a first-order change, they knew they would feel lonely until they could extend this change to the system. Yet, in spite of their loneliness, their future orientation caused them to embrace change optimistically as a valuable developmental possibility.

Their resistance was no longer directed toward me, toward each other, or even toward the educational system. It clearly was channeled toward agency. Resistance had become a creative force allowing them to connect with their own selves, to envision themselves as different, and to see the writing process from the perspective of their students. The teachers had constructed firm images of their own identity and were able to hold fast to them, in spite of the way they were viewed by others.

TEACHER LEARNING THROUGH CONVERSATION

In this chapter I offered both a structural and a thematic analysis of four significant events of discourse-mediated teachers' learning. In the structural analysis, two turns of exposure and risk taking followed by reflective assessment were identified as the basic pattern of learning events illustrated in the four excerpts from this group's discussions. Although this chapter does not attempt to map the progressive trail of growth in these learning events, the chronologically sequenced transcripts show that the structure of the event itself was gradually refined. In the earliest event, the risk taker and the reflective assessor could be identified, but they had a limited impact on the group's thinking. The risk taker initiated the event and the reflective assessor picked up the risk taker's challenge, but they did not manage to start a reframing process within the group. In the second event, the risk taker was an outsider. Right from the start, there was a conflict between her and the group, which started them on a reframing route. The problem she posed triggered a critique by the reflective assessor of the old point of view, which, in turn, caused the other members to reflect upon their own viewpoints. In the third event, the risk taker was again a member of the group. This time her impact was strong and she carried on the argumentation throughout the event. In the fourth event, the teachers who spoke served as both risk takers and reflective assessors. Collaboratively, without facing a conflict, through storytelling, they managed to construct and elaborate different angles of the same viewpoint.

The thematic analysis, focusing on resistance and connecting, traced the different ways in which the two concepts are interrelated. The teachers joined the program in order to fulfill their need to connect and to act. Yet they resisted the particular view of connecting and acting presented in the course, since it seemed to deny their agency. As the locus of their resistance gradually shifted from their learning tasks to more distant issues, they began to reflect on their initial resistance and their own need to connect to their students. The analysis illustrates the processes whereby resistance and connecting created in them the sense of agency for themselves, for students, and for their colleagues. In an unsolicited way, while attempting to deal with the program tasks, the teachers channeled their resistance into dealing with some of the most important issues in writing instruction:

- The relationship between the written product and the writing process
- The difference between control and ownership in learning and teaching
- The analogy between their learning and their students' learning, and the conflict between their values and those of the system in which they function

- The conflict between objectivity and subjectivity in assessing the situation
- The relationship between their professional problems and those of other professionals
- The relationship between self-awareness and change

The more advanced these teachers became in their growth process, the more they reflected on their own process of change, expressing interest in becoming agents of change for other practitioners.

All of these findings emphasize the importance of conversation to teachers' professional development. They show that conversations "do not simply express the underlying fabric of their social world, but are the very processes by which that fabric is created and sustained" (Sampson, 1993, p. 99). Furthermore, teacher conversation not only supports meaning making about present events, but it also helps teachers form visions of the future. In the context of working with teachers on a complex representation of knowledge, whereby the notion of objective "truth" is no longer relevant, conversation creates a space where professional knowledge can be constantly and consciously reframed and reaffirmed.

In this particular study, conversation is more than an important medium for teachers' knowledge construction; it is also a space for teachers to conduct themselves as transformative intellectuals who take risks and struggle against overly simplistic notions of educational change. When conversation takes such a form, resistance can become a catalyst for reframing and also for the growth of a sense of agency toward oneself and toward society.

But creating the space for conversation is not easy. Very often, conversation is not what teachers want. Even teachers who want to change usually expect professional development to present to them "objective" theoretical knowledge and techniques. There is often initial resistance on their part toward the organizers' efforts to engage them in tasks that will help them reflect on their own teaching. It takes some time (in this case, a year) for participants in programs that make space for conversation to begin to revise their expectations about professional development, to challenge existing notions of teachers' learning, and to reflect on their own self-transformation.

REFERENCES

Allen, J., Cary, M., & Delgado, L. (1996). *Exploring blue highways: Literacy reform, school change, and the creation of learning communities.* New York: Teachers College Press.

Atwell, N. (1987). *In the middle: Writing, reading and learning with adolescents.* Upper Montclair, NJ: Boynton/Cook.

Bruner, D. (1992). Teacher resistance and the construction of more educative texts. *Teacher Education, 4*(2), 97–106.

Burbules, N. C., & Rice, S. (1991). Dialogue across differences: Continuing the conversation. *Harvard Educational Review, 61*(4), 393–416.

Clift, R. T., Houston, W. R., & Pugach, M. C. (Eds.). (1990). *Encouraging reflective practice in education.* New York: Teachers College Press.

Cochran-Smith, M. (1991). Learning to teach against the grain. *Harvard Educational Review, 61*(3), 279–310.

Cooper, C. R. (1977). Holistic evaluation of writing. In C. R. Cooper & L. Odell (Eds.), *Evaluating writing* (pp. 3–31). Urbana, IL: National Council of Teachers of English.

Daniels, H., & Zemelman, S. (1985). *A writing project: Training teachers of composition from kindergarten to college.* Portsmouth, NH: Heinemann.

Frake, C. O. (1997). Plying frames can be dangerous. In M. Cole, Y. Engestrom, & O. Valesquez (Eds.), *Mind, culture, and activity* (pp. 32–46). Cambridge, MA: Harvard University Press.

Giddens, A. (1991). *Modernity and self-identity: Self and society in the late modern age.* Stanford: Stanford University Press.

Giroux, H. A. (1988). *Teachers as intellectuals.* New York: Bergin & Garvey.

Grumet, M. R. (1988). *Bitter milk: Women and teaching.* Amherst: University of Massachusetts Press.

Hargreaves, A. (1994). *Changing teachers, changing times.* New York: Teachers College Press.

Haroutunian-Gordon, S. (1991). *Turning the soul: Teaching through conversation in the high school.* Chicago: University of Chicago Press.

Johnston, M. (1997). *Contradictions in collaborations: New thinking on school/university partnership.* New York: Teachers College Press.

Lester, N. B., & Onore, C. S. (1990). *Learning change.* Portsmouth, NH: Boynton/Cook.

Mahoney, M. A., & Yngvesson, B. (1992). The construction of subjectivity and the paradox of resistance: Reintegrating feminist anthropology and psychology. *Signs, 18*(1), 44–73.

Miller, J. L. (1990). *Creating spaces and finding voices.* Albany: State University of New York Press.

Paris, C. L. (1993). *Teacher agency and curriculum making in classrooms.* New York: Teachers College Press.

Pollard, A. (1993). Learning in primary schools. In H. Daniels (Ed.), *Charting the agenda: Educational activity after Vygotsky* (pp. 171–189). London: Routledge.

Roemer, M. G. (1991). What we talk about when we talk about school reform. *Harvard Educational Review, 61*(4), 434–448.

Rogoff, B. (1995). Sociocultural activity on three planes. In J. V. Wertsch, P. Del Rio, & A. Alvarez (Eds.), *Sociocultural studies of mind* (pp. 139–164). New York: Cambridge University Press.

Sampson, E. E. (1993). *Celebrating the other.* Hertfordshire: Harvester Wheatsheaf.

Schön, A. D. (1987). *Educating the reflective practitioner.* San Francisco: Jossey-Bass.
Schön, A. D. (1988). Coaching reflective teaching. In P. P. Grimmett & G. L. Erickson (Eds.), *Reflection in teacher education* (pp. 19–30). Vancouver, BC: Pacific Educational Press.
Schön, A. D. (1991). *The reflective turn: Case studies in and on educational practice.* New York: Teachers College Press.
Swanson-Owens, D. (1986). Identifying natural sources of resistance: A case study of implementing writing across the curriculum. *Research in the Teaching of English, 20,* 69–97.
Vygotsky, S. L. (1978). *Mind in society.* Cambridge, MA: Harvard University Press.
Watzlawick, P., Weakland, J. H., & Fish, R. (1974). *Change: Principles of problem formation and problem resolution.* New York: Norton.
Wertsch, J. V. (1985). *Vygotsky and the social formation of mind.* Cambridge, MA: Harvard University Press.

CHAPTER 4

Reading Lives: Learning About Culture and Literacy in Teacher Study Groups

**Susan Florio-Ruane & Taffy E. Raphael
with the assistance of the Teachers
Learning Collaborative**

T HE ISOLATION WITHIN which contemporary teachers work is so common as to be almost transparent. Isolated from other professionals, teachers and their practice are embedded within a hierarchical system in which the day-to-day activities are governed by external forces: administrative mandates, parental requests, and legislative directives. The teachers—the ones with the most knowledge about the specifics of the contexts in which they work—may feel the least empowered to engage in innovative practices that could enhance the lives of their students in important ways. This chapter is about teacher study groups as activity settings where teachers might break free of that isolation and engage in powerful learning about culture and literacy.

While relatively new to teacher education, women's study groups are embedded in a relatively long tradition in the United States (Gere, 1997). Such groups arise at the margins of more public, official policies and practices and have their genesis in the realities of participants' day-to-day lives. They provide an opportunity for teachers to voice beliefs and concerns, exchange ideas with others, and engage in inquiry about means for enhancing their own lives and the lives of those with whom they work. Study groups provide an activity setting in which these voices and views can be expressed as part of learning.

One issue facing teachers today and about which their voices are infrequently heard is that of culture and the growing diversity of the pupil population of the United States. This diversity stands in contrast to a notable lack of apparent diversity in the teaching force. For many reasons, which we discuss later, current efforts of professional development featuring multicultural education in general, and literacy as cultural practice specifically, fall depressingly short. Some teacher education efforts actually may serve to reinforce the very stereotypes they seek to eliminate. A second issue relates to challenges arising from asking teachers to teach in ways they themselves have never experienced. Current methods grounded in "conversation-based learning" (e.g., literature circles and book clubs, collaborative learning, leading instructional conversations) are rarely part of teachers' own learning experiences.

The topic of culture and the idea of studying it in the company of one's peers require a sustained professional development experience. They require that participants grow in trust, explore a complex idea by repeated passes through it from diverse perspectives, and weave into the exploration a variety of texts, including their own experiences and those of others. In this chapter we describe a 3-year line of research designed to address these two problems in teacher education and professional development. From 1995 through 1997, we researched two study group contexts for teacher learning. The first was a master's course for teachers on culture, literacy, and autobiography; the second was the Literary Circle, a voluntary book club that developed from the course. This voluntary book club continued for 2 years, its conversations spanning 24 books selected by its members.

Our study of the activity settings and participants' conversations in the course and the book club led to our theorizing about the meaning of "sustain" and "sustainable" when referring to teacher development in study groups. Thus, in the chapter, we begin with a description of our research into the two study groups, as well as the underlying rationale for our thematic focus and the value placed on conversation within the study group. We then shift our focus to a discussion of sustainability in light of the groups' described activities and subsequent initiatives.

RESEARCHING THE STUDY GROUPS

The context of both the course and the Literary Circle stressed reading and discussion of ethnic autobiographical literature. In the first, the authors, who are university-based teacher educators and researchers, largely directed this experience. However, with the subsequent formation of the Literary Circle, the participating teachers took more control and responsibility for learning within the group. As participant observers, we worked collaboratively with teachers in the course and in the Literary Circle to read and talk about literature and document the group meetings.

We used ethnographic and sociolinguistic methods to study participants' learning as they read, wrote, and talked about compelling personal literature describing cultural experience. We were interested in teacher learning about both culture and literacy instruction. The study addressed two challenges in contemporary American teacher education: (1) the disparity in background between a largely European-American teaching force and the diverse pupils it serves; and (2) the difficulty of teaching about literacy and culture in responsive, dialogic ways.

Why Culture? Why Conversation?

Literacy is deeply rooted in cultural experience, and our society presents teachers with a broad and rich diversity of youngsters whose cultural experience may differ considerably from their own. Yet, being members of the so-called "mainstream" and trained within a profession linguistically and socially homogeneous, many teachers find themselves culturally isolated. They lack awareness of the cultural foundations of literacy in their own lives as well as in the lives of others. It is difficult for them to investigate complex issues of race, culture, social class, and language diversity. Their professional education typically does not foster in them a sense of culture as a dynamic process whereby people make meaning in contact with one another. By introducing and researching teacher-led book discussions of ethnic literature, we hoped to investigate alternative texts and contexts for teachers to learn about the cultural foundations of literacy in their own and others' lives.

Our study also was designed to investigate the role these alternative texts and contexts might play in improving teachers' learning about literacy instruction. This second goal stems from contemporary expectations that teachers will innovate to improve youngsters' literacy development by making instruction more responsive and dialogic. This typically involves changes in the following:

1. *Textual materials*—moving from commercially prepared short stories and text excerpts as a basis for instruction to using original literature

2. *Curriculum organization*—moving from isolated instruction in reading, writing, language, and subject matter to intra- and interdisciplinary teaching
3. *Roles and contexts*—the teacher moving from controlling topics and turns to assuming a supportive instructional role, while students take greater responsibility for topic selection, discussion, and assessing their own progress

Both the challenge to teach about culture and the challenge to teach responsively are rooted in the paradox of expecting teachers to teach in ways unlike the ways they were taught. Scholars criticize the form and content of professional education for exhorting teachers to foster learning that is dialogic in nature and aimed at framing and solving complex problems, yet rarely providing teachers opportunities to experience such teaching and learning for themselves. To respond to this challenge, we created and studied a dialogic, literature-based form of professional development. One of the teachers who participated in our study registered her interest in this possibility as follows:

One of the most important [reasons for participating] for me was . . . as a teacher . . . because it gave me a feeling for what the kids are trying to do in the classroom. Whenever I participate in things my kids do, it gives me a lot more insight [into] what they're trying to do. (Interview, July 1996)

Details of the Study

Our study combined two prior lines of research. The first focuses on the use of narrative, specifically ethnic autobiography, as a resource for teacher learning about culture (Florio-Ruane with deTar, in press). The second focuses on the pedagogical power of reading, writing, and talking about literature in peer-led book clubs to foster youngsters' comprehension and critical thinking (McMahon & Raphael, with Goatley & Pardo, 1997). We reasoned from these lines of work that teacher-led book club discussions might provide a strategic site in which to foster and investigate teachers' own professional development. We asked the following three research questions:

1. What is the nature of the teachers' oral and written participation in book club activities?

2. How does participation influence their understandings of literacy—its cultural foundations as well as the process of learning from literature?
3. How does their participation inform teacher thinking about literacy curriculum and instruction?

The study began in fall 1995, with support from the National Council of Teachers of English Small Grants program, and continued through summer 1997. The 10 teacher participants in the first teacher study group—the master's course—were typical of both the student cohort at Michigan State University and the national teaching force in that they were European-American, female, monolingual speakers of English, and from lower- and middle-income backgrounds (Gay, 1993). The course instructor (Florio-Ruane) selected the initial six books to be read. Members of the Literary Circle selected the rest, with teachers assuming increasing control of book selection. As a text set (Calkins, 1991) that developed over time, the books explored identity and power at the group and the individual level. Their authors recount what is lost and what is gained when, upon entering American schooling and public society, they are asked to acquire not only new skills and linguistic operations, but also new perspectives on the world and themselves within it.

The participant observers included the authors and four research assistants (Mary McVee, Jocelyn Glazier, Susan Wallace-Cowell, and Bette Shellhorn). This team of researchers documented the activities that took place in the master's course and subsequent book club in five ways: (1) the course instructor maintained an *instructor's journal* detailing her weekly observations of the class and her ongoing questions, concerns, and instructional decisions; (2) the researchers engaged as participant observers in the course and Literary Circle, writing *field notes* immediately after each meeting; (3) all book discussions were *audiotaped* and two were also *videotaped* for analysis; (4) *written texts* produced by the teachers were collected and studied; and (5) all teachers were *interviewed* about the book club experience in both the course and the Literary Circle.

Data collection and analysis used techniques drawn from ethnography and sociolinguistics, including: (1) the gradual refinement of research questions and the inductive development of analytic categories grounded in continuous comparison of data as they were collected (Glaser & Strauss, 1967); (2) triangulation among different kinds and sources of data to cross-check inferences about participants' understandings (Gordon, 1980); and (3) collaborative analysis of conversations, interviews, and written texts for insights into the ways participants represented their ideas and negotiated them in social interaction with others (Denyer & Florio-Ruane, 1995).

WHAT WE LEARNED THROUGH SUSTAINED TEACHER INQUIRY

Our project was premised on the idea that learning begins and ends on the social plane (Harre, 1984). Approaching this work with a social historical lens, we developed a descriptive analysis highlighting changes in participants' ways of communicating with one another about the autobiographies, their own literary and cultural backgrounds, and their work as teachers. We took these changes in discursive practices as evidence of changes in participants' thinking about culture and also about reading and responding to literature (Gavelek & Raphael, 1996). Our findings about teachers' learning are described below within four broad categories: the role of a study group network, the role of narrative, the role of conversation, and teachers' intellectual identity development within a context of conversation and sustained inquiry.

The Role of a Study Group Network

Teachers' response to autobiographical literature in the course and in the Literary Circle played a primary role in shaping their learning. Teachers often responded to the autobiographies by telling personal stories. Analyzing personal narratives told in response to the published autobiographies helped us understand how participants viewed their own life experiences in contrast to those encountered in literature. This was a critical step in the exploration of diversity and difference, and it set the stage for one important contribution to sustainability—personal connection to the participants' professional lives.

The study groups became the contexts in which these important ideas were explored and applied to participants' own teaching and their school community. Thus professional growth did not depend on the school faculty as the unit of experience, nor was the teacher viewed as an isolate, changing her practice apart from colleagues. Moreover, the isolation of teachers in communities disparate in region, socioeconomic standing, language, ethnic characteristics, and so forth, is bridged by the participation of teachers from different schools and communities. Finally, electronic technologies such as the Internet and e-mail facilitate this crossing of borders, supporting and sustaining conversation even when participants cannot be present face-to-face (Raphael et al., 2000).

The Role of Narrative in Teachers' Learning

Recently, psychologists, anthropologists, and literary theorists have focused much attention on the power of narrative to define or redefine self and other. Yet even as the potential exists for narrative to be a powerful tool in exploring and transforming identity, stories are also limited, particularly when told within conversation (Tannen, 1989). While embedding personal narrative in conversation allowed participants to share views, it also constrained them. For example, narratives told by the European-American, middle-class women in our study were typically brief, composed of a few key events tied to a general summary, and often connected thematically with one another. Their length, structure, and content functioned to sustain conversational involvement in the group. The pattern was familiar and comfortable.

However, participants reported in debriefing interviews that these cooperative narrative patterns of discourse, while enjoyable, sometimes precluded their telling of longer, more complex personal narratives or ones they felt did not resonate with the emerging group theme (McVee, 1999). In this sense, the forms and function of the narratives inhibited exploration of issues of diversity or difference. An example from a master's course book club discussion serves to illustrate. It is drawn from participant observation research on the book club by Mary McVee (Florio-Ruane, with deTar, in press; Glazier et al., 2000).

McVee, who had grown up on a ranch in Montana, participated in a book club discussion of Jill Ker Conway's autobiography, *The Road from Coorain* (1989), with teachers who had grown up in Michigan. Coorain is a sheep ranch in the Australian outback, and Conway's family is forced to leave the family ranch because of a severe drought. Coorain is a central metaphor in Conway's autobiography of her life in rural and urban Australia and her coming of age as a woman and scholar. The book club members talked about Coorain, drawing on their own lived experiences. Several teachers in the group grew up on dairy farms in Michigan. Connections were made readily among participants across a myriad of agricultural contexts—from dairy farming to ranching to backyard gardening.

Several participants spoke of their experiences growing up on farms. In the following example reported by McVee (in Glazier et al., 2000), we see two participants exchange turns smoothly, each linking her turn topically with what has been said previously, thus weaving a sense of shared understanding and interpersonal connection. Each has grown up in a farming context, and each sees that experience to be connected to her understanding of Conway's autobiography. Here they are talking about the farmer's consciousness of weather:

SPEAKER 1: Well, I know just the, what the nature and the weather thing.
SPEAKER 2: Yeah, that affected me because being on a farm, where what your dad is able to do and his farm hands in the course of the day

has to do with the weather. You know and what you're gonna be
able to accomplish in that day and, you know, it's all around the
weather. The connection between nature.
SPEAKER 1: I find myself even now, you know, like being very conscious
of how many sunny days we've had in a row.
SPEAKER 2: Me too.
SPEAKER 1: And how many rainy days we've had in a row.
SPEAKER 2: How are the farmers doing? (p. 310)

There is a high degree of involvement in the speakers' talk—completing one another's sentences, noting agreement, repeating one another's key words or themes. One way to view this example is that participants are forming a kind of connected knowing in which they respond to Conway's text and to one another with narratives elaborating key themes in the book. This can be viewed as a framing and focusing on meaning that is essential to comprehension. However, it also can be viewed, as it was by McVee, as a "narrowing" of focus—a premature assumption of understanding on the part of the speakers, such that they gloss over differences in context and meaning in the service of continuity and consensus.

Because their families did not have to grow their own food for the dairy cattle, these speakers did not share Conway's desperate experience of watching livestock starve to death because of drought. One of the graduate students working as a participant observer in the course experienced this as a move that limited her own and others' opportunity to learn from the narratives by means of comparison and contrast. Mary McVee grew up on a ranch in Montana. Its isolation, expansiveness, and dependence on climate closely resembled Conway's description of Coorain. Like Conway, McVee lived through her family's near loss of its land because of drought. She viewed the prevailing teacher interpretation as limiting the ways in which Conway's work might be understood and wanted the group to acknowledge that, in her words, "a ranch is not a dairy farm."

Although McVee wanted the group to struggle with the differences as a starting point for talking about their responses to Coorain and the drought as central metaphors in Conway's autobiography, she did not introduce this alternative into the conversation. Not wanting to disrupt the conversation's apparent coherence and participants' congeniality, McVee remained silent. She noted her frustration with the conversation later and in writing—first in her personal journal and then in a study of the conversation's dynamics—analyzing "what went wrong" in this discussion from her point of view.

One can imagine other, similar problems with book club discussion—for example, where readings of Conway's book might be undertaken by city dwellers whose sole experience with agriculture was a small window garden. The point is not to assert one "correct" reading of the metaphor but to suggest that the narratives we read—and the narrative responses participants made to them—were not inherently instructive about difference and diversity. They could be strung together thematically to suggest connection and shared knowledge or they might be read in terms of their difference, thus shedding light on differences in participants' experiences, prior knowledge, or social position. Lack of awareness of these possibilities limits the educative potential of narratives.

Mary McVee's reluctance to point out that a ranch is not a dairy farm and the students' response to her silence illustrate and reinforce a general pattern in the conversations, especially in the course, where participants lacked familiarity with book clubs, the theme of culture, the genre of autobiography, and one another. Conversation was biased toward thematic, structural, and social connection with others. This is a typical, preferred style of conversation documented by researchers who have studied the conversation and learning of middle-class, Caucasian females in the United States—very much the people who fill the ranks of the teaching profession in our country (Belenky, Clinchy, Goldberger, & Tarule, 1986; Edelsky, 1993).

Absent other voices at the table, and even admitting of within-group diversity (as is the case in McVee's example), the force of politeness and consensus is strong and may go unnoticed and unexamined. Thus, while potentially empowering for some of the speakers, study group conversation, and its embedded, connected, and uncontested narratives, can reinforce, even reify, an uncritical assumption of homogeneity and limit exploration of even modest differences in knowledge, perspective, or values. In short, while personal narrative played an important role in facilitating book club discussion, it also limited participants' exploration of difference both among themselves and between themselves and the authors of the published autobiographies.

These findings raise important questions for further research about how narrative, particularly in multicultural classrooms and curriculum, can support or make manifest participants' learning about difference (McVee, 1999). They also point to the limits and the possibilities of conversation as an activity setting within which teachers can learn about culture and diversity.

Conversation About "Hot Lava" Topics

Our research enabled us to think about how to expand the cultural consciousness of so-called "White teachers" (Paley, 1979/1989). Through their involvement in 2 years of book club conversations, we learned a great deal from our collaborating teachers about the conditions that seem to support critical talk about culture and some of the difficult issues it encompasses (e.g., inequality based on race, language, ethnicity, and gender).

At the beginning of our project, what was particularly evident in participants' talk was a sense of "culturelessness." One teacher said in a debriefing interview after a year of participation, "I was one of those people in the beginning who [thought] I had no culture. There's nothing to me. I've had no experiences." This comment resonates with work in the field of cultural studies, which asserts that members of the so-called "dominant culture" hold taken-for-granted assumptions of an amorphous monoculturalism (Frankenburg, 1993) and a stance of "color blindness" (Paley, 1979/1989). This social positioning limits their reflection upon and discussion of race, racism, privilege, and Whiteness (MacIntyre, 1997).

Along with this stance comes an informal, unspoken "code of ethics" that denotes how the topic of race should be engaged in public spaces. As the novelist and literary critic Toni Morrison (1992) suggests, "In matters of race, silence and evasion have historically ruled" discourse (p. 9). In analyzing conversations in the book club, particularly those about African American authors and their texts, we found evidence of this silence. We also found evidence that, over time and by means of intertextual experiences, participants became gradually more willing to engage difficult topics like race as they became familiar with one another, with book club as an activity, and with diverse authors and texts.

This finding is illustrated by our analysis of conversations around two works by Maya Angelou, *I Know Why the Caged Bird Sings* (1969), read and discussed early in the master's course, and *Gather Together in My Name* (1974), read later, after the course ended and participants formed a voluntary book club. Jocelyn Glazier, a participant observer, chose to analyze talk in these two contexts because, unlike the smoothly linked exchanges in more typical conversations such as the discussion of *The Road from Coorain*, talk about Angelou's books seemed to be more difficult to focus and sustain. Glazier wondered why this might be the case and undertook extensive analysis of these two book club conversations. Among the many things that stand out in these books is their confronting of the reader with difficult, edgy topics—often in a folkloric style and always to provoke the expectations of European American readers (Lionnet, 1989).

What is evident from Glazier's analysis of these two conversations, spaced approximately 6 months apart, is that difficult topics raised by Angelou were avoided initially in book club conversation. Of this Glazier writes that "conversations about topics such as racism, sexual assault, and social class—all raised in Angelou's books—are among those difficult for these book club participants to sustain" (Glazier et al., 2000, p. 296). Glazier came to call topics such as these "hot lava." Like the children's playground game, where the goal is to run a course yet avoid stepping on spots of "hot lava," book club participants initially tended to approach and then dart away from difficult topics in their conversational interplay. However, despite their efforts, these topics did not go away.

The autobiographical literature we read (and the personae of its diverse authors) was a persistent reminder of these topics. And in the case of some, such as Maya Angelou, the author was a ubiquitous figure in American popular as well as literary culture, whose voice continued to insinuate itself into the group. Participants had multiple "Maya sightings" on television, in books, on the radio, and in newspapers. These built a sense of kinship with Angelou, and they began to evoke her and some of the more difficult themes her books address. The "hot lava" accumulated in the other books and authors read over the 2 years of the Literary Circle's life span. Participants revisited Angelou's writing, seeking links to and differences from the writings of other African American female authors (e.g., Zora Neale Hurston, Toni Morrison, and Alice Walker), African American male authors (e.g., James McBride), as well as authors both male and female from other times, places, and ethnic groups (e.g., Amy Tan, Mike Rose, Jung Chang, Esmeralda Santiago, Frank McCourt, Mary Crow Dog, and Victor Villasenor).

This intertextual encounter with "hot lava" themes such as racism and inequality increased fluency with ideas and trust among conversants. It shed light on within-group differences, intergroup similarities and differences, and the importance of both local and historical context. It led us beyond stereotyped readings of isolated books, seeking instead the thematic connections among books and the way in which taking multiple passes at an idea could increase our understanding of that idea as well as our ability to sustain difficult talk about it. We were, for example, initially unable to articulate how, in *Their Eyes Were Watching God* (Hurston, 1937), the oppression of African American men and women in the post-Reconstruction American South might have caused profound stress in their relationships with one another. It was far easier to critique individual characters' motives or temperament than to sense the ways in which these were socially, politically, and culturally situated.

With the accumulation of talk and texts, however, the group began to draw comparisons and contrasts. It was easier for us to examine the historical, social, and political dimensions of oppression in distant societies and cultures such as China than in familiar ones like our own. Reading

The Wild Swans (Chang, 1991), for example, we were easily and deeply moved by the author's account of the damaging effects oppressive political systems had on the Chinese family. Using descriptions of more distant lives and places as touchstones, we re-read Hurston's work in a different way, tackling the more difficult task of considering (and reconsidering) racism's impact on individual and family identity. Our research suggests that this willingness to risk did not, however, come easily or quickly. It took 2 long years. Only with sufficient time to negotiate a shared identity as members of the book club did participants appear to break their silence and create for themselves a new "curriculum" for thinking and speaking about what, for Caucasian and middle-class Americans, are historically difficult topics. This finding speaks to the challenge of teacher professional development in the area of culture.

Professional development in the area of cultural diversity is notoriously challenging, both because it is difficult for teachers to talk about "hot lava" topics and because most inservice education is of short duration. Time limits both context and text such that teachers typically learn about "others" by studying the characteristics of ethnic groups in texts (both oral and written) where expert knowledge is presented to them. Lacking opportunities to explore culture as a complex and lived process in which everyone participates, and lacking time to garner cultural understanding in and through multiple, complex, multivoiced texts, teachers tend to come away from such professional development reinforced in their extant beliefs and prejudices (McDiarmid & Price, 1990). What seems needed, instead, is multicultural education not as a set of techniques or discrete factual content, but as a process of critical engagement—with self, others, texts, and ideas (Chavez Chavez & O'Donnell, 1998).

Teachers' Intellectual Identity

Our research on the study groups examined participants' views of their own learning and professional growth, drawing primarily on analysis of interview data and personal writing done by the teachers as part of course and book club participation. The teachers reported learning about aspects of identity, including professional practice, personal intellectual growth, and participation in literacy as culturally grounded practice. While we had hypothesized that they would learn about literacy and culture, a key unanticipated finding was that teachers reported discovering themselves as "thinkers" as a result of their involvement in book discussions.

Repeatedly, teachers talked of the impact that book club reading and conversations had on their sense of professional agency. Specific references were made to creating book club groups within their school settings; presenting their curriculum work locally to colleagues within their school, in their district, and at state and national conferences; and continuing to enhance their own intellectual lives by reading multicultural literature. Analyzing the teachers' writing and interviews, we gained insight into this sense of agency. We identified four clear themes: (1) increased confidence in and expression of their ideas; (2) a new tendency to envision alternative "possible selves" as they thought about their futures as teachers and as citizens; (3) increased desire to pursue learning; and (4) a renewed passion for literature and its ideas. The opportunity to read challenging literature, talk about it with colleagues, and craft (and hear) one another's personal narratives enhanced teachers' sense of themselves not only as teachers, but as thoughtful participants in society.

SUSTAINABILITY AS A FEATURE OF
LEARNING CONVERSATIONS

As the teachers' identity as professionals who have agency increased and as their critical analysis of the current school curriculum became more sophisticated, we began to understand why and how the book club sustained itself and became progressively more intimate. There was an energy in the teachers' work lives that was traceable to their desire to apply what they had learned about themselves in their own teaching. The continued interactions around curricula that they wanted to enact may have provided some of the impetus to continue to stay together. This finding also illustrates some ideas about how to sustain a group.

In sustainable groups, the goals may shift. As early efforts toward one goal come to fruition, doors open to new goals that can serve to keep a group going, even with the inevitable departures of some of its members. In short, while the participants move in and out of involvement, the evolving practices and knowledge of the group continue to be invoked, in the case of our study group, over 24 book club meetings and 24 books about culture, education, and identity.

One of the benefits of this kind of sustainable growth is that, in studying the idea of "culture," it is possible for difference to be identified and for conversations in, through, and about difference to unfold. Especially in a profession that remains primarily Caucasian, English-speaking, female, and middle income, it is far too easy to (1) rationalize the sources of difference between teachers and pupils; (2) treat culture as something "others" have and we do not; (3) treat European-American experience as "normal" or unmarked and other ethnic experiences as "abnormal" or marked; and (4) assume a homogeneity in the teaching force that ignores important experiences of difference among ourselves and thus makes it hard to see how our own cultural practices and positions are socially and historically determined.

Over time in the Literary Circle participants identified and elaborated differences in their own coming of age as participants in culture and, by extension, their experience of schooling and the process of becoming literate. It became easier and more interesting for participants to craft their own "literacy narratives" (Soliday, 1994). In these stories, the teller captures aspects of coming of age within a particular community, tradition, and family by describing the kinds of texts and literacy events encountered or created there. One teacher, Kate, developed a project for herself (extended ultimately to her development of a curriculum project for youngsters) in which she culled "artifacts" of her own coming of age as a woman, a Catholic, and the daughter of farmers. She brought to this documentary work a close analysis of personal books, photographs, and writings. It is significant that literacy played a prominent role in Kate's project, in the books we read, in the stories many of us told, and in the study group's practice. In many ways we embodied in the study group the idea that literacy is itself a cultural practice and that each learner brings personal literacy narratives to the table as we talk about literacy education.

The aim of the study group was not sustainability, but its evolving practices and problems occasioned its having the kind of duration and focus that it ultimately had. This was an experience that was not paid for by large research grants, was not convened and determined by professors, did not compensate members in money or status, did not take place during "work time" or within the walls of members' workplaces, and was not about the day-to-day concerns of classroom teachers. Why, then, did members come so faithfully to participate in discussions of literature and link that participation to their growth as thinkers, citizens, and educators?

EXTENSIONS INTO PRACTICE

If we accept a model of sociocognitive development in which learning occurs and is evidenced by engagement with others (who are alternately peers and more experienced others), we can look for evidence in our study of learning not only on the part of teachers, but also among the project's teacher educator/researchers. We identified the following five domains of learning-oriented change occasioned by our collaboration: (1) defining the book club situation; (2) shaping the thematic content of book club talk and text; (3) defining culture in more complex ways; (4) transforming ways of talking and ways of reading; and (5) reaching out to professional communities and classrooms. Each will be touched on briefly below.

When we stepped back from the study group to reflect on its life history, we found increased leadership among the teachers over time and a shift in teacher educator/researchers' participation from project leader/ initiators to fellow club members. As the circle of leadership widened, changes occurred in decision making about what to read, why to read, and how to read.

The multiple voices within the group discursively crafted an emergent, open-ended "syllabus" reaching far beyond the one with which the course began. It took the form of an expanding network of linked texts (both oral and written) that were read differently (primarily by citing and referring to texts in different ways over time—moving from the explicitly personal or critical/descriptive to a hybrid of these two ways of reading). We found that learning in the study group spanned exploring the complexity of culture, confronting difficult topics (especially race and racism), learning to construe reading as a dialogic process of making meaning in response to text and within interpretive communities, and viewing culture as intimately tied to education for literacy.

Out of this learning, we gradually widened the circle to make three kinds of extensions into practice. These extensions took the following forms and, in fact, continue, with some of the same participants plus newer members: curriculum development for pupils; annotated bibliography; teacher support networks; public presentations about the group and what is being learned within it, and members tracking and documenting their own learning within this experience—both to enhance their understanding of what has been happening to them and to learn how this experience might be shared with other teachers and with pupils in productive ways. These sorts of learning experiences tend not to be readily available to teachers in their ordinary work or in typical staff development. Yet they resemble the higher-order learning experiences teachers are expected to cultivate in youngsters.

Extensions from the study groups into practice have led to the development of a network of teacher researchers working in Michigan in diverse communities and school settings to continue the conversation about culture, literacy, and autobiography. This network is an example of the evolution of a study group so that it can encompass new members and grow with the ideas their participation brings. Further, we have taken our learning—both in form and in content—into our classrooms, trying to seed the curriculum and instructional environment with opportunities for youngsters to participate in similarly sustainable and peer-led explorations of culture and its textual representations.

The experience of the network leaves us with new questions that we are continuing to explore together as a form of conversation-based teacher development. We are investigating, for example, the ways in which teachers who have had a chance to participate in such an experience might approach literacy instruction differently from colleagues who have not had this experience. We are researching the development of curricula for youngsters that make room for this kind of sustained and dialogic study of text within an array of potentially competing demands and models for instruction proffered in the name of reform.

We currently are studying together what we think makes a good teacher of literacy, treating our network as a platform for looking critically at national standards to which policy makers believe teachers of literacy should be held. In this way we are continuing our own professional conversation and, in so doing, trying to engage a wider conversation about teaching and teachers.

NOTES

This research was supported by a grant from the National Council of Teachers of English. It also was supported in part under the Educational Research and Development Center Program, PR/Award Number R305R70004, as administered by the Office of Educational Research and Improvement, U.S. Department of Education. The comments contained in this report do not necessarily reflect the positions, policies, or endorsement of the federal government or the National Institute of Student Achievement, Curriculum, and Assessment, or of the National Institute on Early Childhood Development, or of the U.S. Department of Education.

The Teachers Learning Collaborative (TLC) is a network of teachers that began with the Literary Circle described in this chapter. As the group expanded, it linked three such circles, one in the Lansing, Michigan, area; one in the Oakland, Michigan, area; and one in Detroit, Michigan. Participants in the TLC network who contributed insights to this work include Jocelyn Glazier, Mary McVee, Susan Wallace-Cowell, and Bette Shellhorn, all formerly graduate students at Michigan State University; Andrew Topper, a former postdoctoral fellow at Michigan State; and the following teacher colleagues: Karen Eisele, Marianne George, Kristen Grattan, Nina Hasty, Amy Heitman, Kathy Highfield, Marcella Kehus, Molly Reed, and Jennifer Szlachta.

We are grateful to Christopher Clark for introducing us to the "hot lava" metaphor.

REFERENCES

Angelou, M. (1969). *I know why the caged bird sings*. New York: Bantam Books.

Angelou, M. (1974). *Gather together in my name*. New York: Bantam Books.

Belenky, M. F., Clinchy, B. McV., Goldberger, N. R., & Tarule, J. M. (1986). *Women's ways of knowing: The development of self, voice, and mind*. New York: Basic Books.

Calkins, L. (1991). *Living between the lines*. Portsmouth, NH: Heinemann.

Chang, J. (1991). *The wild swans*. New York: Doubleday.

Chavez Chavez, R., & O'Donnell, J. (1998). *Speaking the unpleasant: The politics of (non)engagement in the multicultural education terrain*. Albany: State University of New York Press.

Conway, J. K. (1989). *The road from Coorain*. New York: Vintage Books.

Denyer, J., & Florio-Ruane, S. (1995). Mixed messages and missed opportunities: Moments of transformation in learning to teach about text. *International Journal of Teaching and Teacher Education, 15*(6), 539–551.

Edelsky, C. (1993). Who's got the floor? In D. Tannen (Ed.), *Gender and conversational interaction* (pp. 189–227). New York: Oxford University Press.

Florio-Ruane, S., with deTar, J. (in press). *Teacher education and the cultural imagination: Autobiography, conversation, and narrative*. Mahwah, NJ: Erlbaum.

Frankenburg, R. (1993). *White women, race matters: The social construction of whiteness*. Minneapolis: University of Minnesota Press.

Gavelek, J. R., & Raphael, T. E. (1996). Changing talk about text: New roles for teachers and students. *Language Arts, 73*, 24–34.

Gay, G. (1993). Building cultural bridges: A bold proposal for teacher education. *Education and Urban Society, 25*(3), 285–299.

Gere, A. R. (1997). *Intimate practices: Literacy and cultural work in US women's clubs 1880–1920*. Urbana: University of Illinois Press.

Glaser, B., & Strauss, A. (1967). *The discovery of grounded theory*. Chicago: Aldine.

Glazier, J., McVee, M., Wallace-Cowell, S., Shellhorn, B., Florio-Ruane, S., & Raphael, T. (2000). Teacher learning in response to autobiographical literature. In N. Karolides (Ed.), *Reader response in secondary and college classrooms* (2nd ed.; pp. 287–310). Mahwah, NJ: Erlbaum.

Gordon, R. L. (1980). *Interviewing: Strategies, techniques, and tactics*. Homewood, IL: Dorsey Press.

Harre, R. (1984). *Personal being: A theory for individual psychology*. Cambridge, MA: Harvard University Press.

Hurston, Zora Neale. (1937). *Their eyes were watching God: A novel*. Philadelphia: Lippincott.

Lionnet, F. (1989). *Autobiographical voices: Race, gender, and self-portraiture*. Ithaca, NY: Cornell University Press.

MacIntyre, A. (1997). *Making meaning of whiteness: Exploring racial identity with white teachers*. Albany: State University of New York Press.

McDiarmid, G. W., & Price, J. (1990). *Prospective teachers' views of diverse learners: A study of participants in the ABCD project* (Technical Report). East Lansing: Michigan State University, Institute for Research on Teacher Education.

McMahon, S. I., & Raphael, T. E., with Goatley, V. J., & Pardo, L. S. (1997). *The book club connection: Exploring alternative contexts for literacy instruction*. New York: Teachers College Press.

McVee, M. B. (1999). *Narrative and the exploration of culture, self, and other in teachers' book club discussion groups*. Unpublished doctoral dissertation, Michigan State University, East Lansing.

Morrison, T. (1992). *Playing in the dark: Whiteness and the literary imagination*. New York: Vintage Books.

Paley, V. (1989). *White teacher*. Cambridge, MA: Harvard University Press. (Original work published 1979)

Raphael, T., George, M., Florio-Ruane, S., Highfield, K., Kehus, M., & Hasty, N. (2000, May 2). *Thinking for ourselves: Literacy in a diverse teacher inquiry network*. Research award address to the International Reading Association, Indianapolis.

Soliday, M. (1994). Translating self and difference through literacy narratives. *College English, 56*(5), 511–526.

Tannen, D. (1989). *Talking voices*. New York: Cambridge University Press.

CHAPTER 5

Learning the Discourse of Teaching: Conversation as Professional Development

Frances Rust & Lily Orland

T HIS CHAPTER CONTINUES and broadens the conversation among teacher educators about who our contemporary students are, what they are capable of doing for themselves (with adequate scaffolding), and how we can constructively blur the arbitrary distinction between preservice teacher preparation and continuing professional development of teachers. Here, we draw on two different but complementary lines of research: Frances Rust's work with a group of teachers as they move from their preservice programs into their first years of teaching, and Lily Orland's study of the development of novice mentors' talk and understanding as they learn to support inservice teachers. Together, we have begun to develop a theory about the way conversations change and deepen among beginners in the field of teaching, between beginners and experienced teachers, and among experienced teachers and mentors.

STRUCTURING OUR INQUIRY

We develop two strands of inquiry in this chapter: to describe what it is that preservice and inservice teachers converse about, and to identify patterns of talk that are associated with different levels of teachers' experience. The data of our inquiry are drawn from stories and narratives that have emerged in conversation groups where each of us has been both participant and observer.

Frances Rust and Susan Haver, a former NYU faculty member, co-facilitate The New Teachers' Conversation Group, a group made up of juniors and seniors, and first-, second-, and third-year teachers—all members or graduates of the undergraduate program in Early Childhood and Elementary Education at New York University. Attendance is entirely voluntary. While the group meets on the average of once a month throughout the year (including summer), it has no fixed meeting schedule. Instead, the date of the next meeting is decided upon as the conversation finishes at the current meeting. Friday evenings have remained the best evening for the group members during the school year. It is a time to relax over dinner together and to share teaching stories. The group has been meeting together for 4 years.

Lily Orland's group consisted of novice and experienced mentors who participated in a master's level course entitled "Mentoring Skills and Practices." Orland taught the course in the Department of Education at the University of Haifa in Israel. The course was structured around the writing and sharing of stories and cases drawn from the mentors' experiences. The 15 participants were all practicing inservice mentors of secondary teachers of a variety of content areas. The participants were from both Jewish and Arab sectors of Israel.

Our inquiry into these conversations has been informed by understandings of story and narrative that draw on the work of Bruner (1990), Florio-Ruane (1991), Schubert (1991), and Witherell and Noddings (1991). We see the stories that new teachers and experienced mentors tell of their lives as student teachers, beginning teachers, and mentors as "acts of meaning" (Bruner, 1990) through which they make sense of the work of teaching. We take the view that conversation around stories and cases from the lived experiences of participants constitutes a powerful tool for fostering teachers' professional growth (Clark, 1995; Connelly & Clandinin, 1995; Elbaz, in press; Florio-Ruane, 1991; Gudmundsdottir, 1997; Kelchtermans, 1993; Van Manen, 1990). With Witherell and Noddings (1991) and Gomez and Tabachnick (1992), we see the stories that these teachers tell as opportunities for discovery, learning, and sense making about themselves and their profession. As such, these stories can be seen

as essential pieces in the construction of a larger narrative about learning
to teach and about teaching itself.

We have used techniques and procedures of grounded theory analysis (Glaser & Strauss, 1967; Strauss & Corbin, 1990) to frame working
hypotheses that we have tested, revised, and refined by comparing conversations from one meeting to another and across the different kinds of
data we collected.

CONVERSATION AMONG PRESERVICE
AND BEGINNING TEACHERS

What do new teachers talk about? Themselves, their students, their teaching, their schools. In the New Teachers Conversation Group at NYU, participants talk about all of these topics in ways that speak of their lived experience as learners and as new teachers who are learning about teaching.
These are teachers who have grown into the profession like children in a
large family. They are all graduates of the same program. Although they
were not all in the same cohort during their preservice years, they share
many of the same experiences, courses, and faculty connections. There is
among us a bond of familiarity and trust that has distinguished this group
from its inception, permitting a frankness that is unusual.

Over 4 years of monthly meetings, I (Frances) have listened to the
talk of these preservice and beginning teachers, and as I have analyzed
my notes from our conversations, I have seen a variety of patterns emerge.
The most obvious of these is that there is a qualitative difference in the
ways preservice teachers talk about themselves and the work of teaching,
compared with the talk of beginning and more experienced teachers.

Defining Self in Conversation

Members of the group who are preservice students use their autobiographies, lived experience, and life as preservice students as referents. They
talk in general terms and of major concepts. Members of the group who
are in their first years of teaching situate themselves as teachers and
talk in specifics to life in classrooms. Take, for example, our very first
conversation group meeting in April 1996:

> We begin with introductions. James is a junior. A 30-year-old un-
> dergraduate, he's had a lot of time to think about teaching and to
> study it. Having tried college several times, James has strong opin-
> ions about good teaching. He says that he can't remember a time

when he didn't want to do this. Growing up in the suburbs of Chicago, he was keenly aware of racism and the power of teachers as leaders. He wants to teach in emancipatory ways to empower students.

Sara is a first-year teacher in a public school in Chinatown. "I am teaching sixth grade," she says. "I have 46 students. I went into teaching because I wanted to help my community. I love this work."

More introductions ensue, and then comes a discussion of problem kids. Rebecca (a senior) can see herself getting authoritarian in the classroom. She feels herself headed for that and she's concerned. She then tells us about a child with an awful voice who gets on her nerves and is not fitting in with the other children. She asks us what to do.

James responds with a story about a difficult child in his class. Patricia (a senior) talks about a child that no one likes.

Sara tells us how she has reached out to a child who does not shower and smells quite bad. She moved the child up to the front of the room right near her desk. She took to spraying air freshener around herself and the child. She talked with the child and arranged for him to bathe in the morning in the sink at school before the other children came. Simultaneously, she talked with the child's mother. She discovered that there was always laundry in the bathtub of their home. Sara, the child, and the mother developed a schedule that went on the fridge at home that enabled the child (and other family members) to use the tub twice a week.

As the years go on, the pattern remains. Preservice teachers worry mostly about and are focused almost exclusively on themselves, while their more experienced peers can "see" children in the complex contexts of their lives (Rust, 1999b). Thus, the conversation of preservice students situates them on a different experiential plane from that of classroom teachers in the group, even from teachers who have been teaching for only a few months.

The Role of Autobiography

Autobiography plays a major role in our conversation; however, it appears in different ways depending on who is talking and where the speakers are in their professional journeys. For those in the group who are in their first years of teaching, autobiography rarely emerges. When it does, it is something that we, as a group, call for, or it is something that is prompted by the conversation and works to situate the speaker as a teacher in a particular setting. In this way, autobiographical stories can provide critical insights into teachers' thinking that work to enable the group not only to understand the speaker's actions but also to provide professional support.

Mari taught me to listen carefully for the autobiographical story. Mari's first year of teaching was in a very difficult school serving low-income families in one of the outer boroughs of New York City. It was not a school that any of us were familiar with. From her first week of teaching, Mari was critical of the children. She talked about them as "delinquents" and was reluctant to do things that others were doing, like share her own library of books with them. She seemed to have forgotten all that she had been taught about guided reading, hands-on math and science, and social studies made relevant to their lives. Instead, according to Mari, her time with her fourth graders was devoted completely to keeping them in their seats and keeping them quiet. In a matter of days, some of the children began to challenge her authority. They refused to do things that she told them to do. At least one called her "bitch." In response to our questions, Mari said that her response was "to ignore those kids." She was following the advice of other teachers in the school who told her this was the way to handle such behavior.

Between September and May, Mari came three times to the conversation group. Each time she came, the story was the same. Only her disdain for the children grew. Her response to our suggestions was a uniform, "It won't work in my school." During this time, she sent e-mail to me and to other members of the teacher education program in which she described the behavior of her students and her "disgust" with them. Like the members of the conversation group, each of us tried to find a way to appeal to Mari's better self and to encourage her to look beyond the students' behavior to what might be motivating it and to what she might do to change the situation. She rejected any suggestions about altering the curriculum or taking advantage of the technology in the classroom. However, she continued to come to the conversation group, albeit after lengthy absences.

In January, Mari told the conversation group members about difficult interactions with fellow teachers that made her feel very alone both personally and professionally. She came to the conversation group, she said, "because you know who I am." We encouraged her to think about moving to another school for the next year.

When she came again in May, Mari seemed relaxed. She anticipated working with kindergartners in the coming year. We expressed surprise that she had decided to stay at the school. On the one hand, she described improved relationships with the other teachers; on the other, she described a class that was in disarray. Since she no longer had the leverage of passing the state tests to help her keep her students in line, Mari was now coping with an unruly class and the mass of paperwork that accompanied decisions about promotion and retention. Her solution was to develop a setup wherein she worked at the front of the room with 12 students (mostly girls) and left the back of the room to five unruly students (mostly boys). When we suggested activities for the boys like computers and drawing, she said they couldn't read and were too hostile for her to spend time with:

> I'm trying to do writing with them but most of them are just crumpling paper. They're not learning anything. They just sit in the corner and play with toys. They're the ones who have been misbehaving since the beginning. I'm just going to hold them over. I don't know what else to do. I have kids who will punch each other out for the computer. One boy says, "I hate you, bitch."

To each suggestion or story that came from a member of the group, Mari had a counter, until David (an experienced teacher) suggested using fourth-grade science material. She responded that science was the one area everyone in her class seemed to like. We probed and then suggested she focus on science activities for the remainder of the year. Her concerns about how far behind her students were started to surface along with her feelings of helplessness in the face of their anger. Stories were told by members of the group about ways that they had handled anger and despair among their students:

> CHRISTIE (first-year teacher): Children who have been abused are very guarded with adults. You have to talk straight to them. You have to let them know that you are a human being.
> MARI: What should I say?
> CHRISTIE: You've really hurt my feelings. I'm not talking to you.
> MARI: I don't know how to do that. All my life, I've been taught to ignore stuff like this. When I was a little girl and got teased about the way I looked [she was the only Asian student in her school], my mom would tell me, "Just ignore them." The teachers all tell me to do the same thing.
> EMILY (first-year teacher, to Christie): If she does that, isn't she showing that she has a weak side, a soft side? [Emily, too, has been told to let such things slide and not to let her emotions show.]

CHRISTIE: That's faulty logic.

JAMES (senior): They need to see another side of you.

CHRISTIE: This is where the "us against them" mentality comes from.

SUSAN HAVER (co-facilitator): If you don't react, you give one of three messages—that it's okay to talk to you and one another like that; that it's not okay, but you're not going to react; or that it's not okay, but you don't care.

The conversation continued in this vein, with increasing evidence provided to Mari to help her move beyond her fear and try engaging with her kids. When I left that evening, I caught a glimpse of Mari and Christie still engaged in intense, authentic talk.

Mari's description of a lifelong pattern had unlocked the door on her resistance, enabling us to negotiate a solution with her that would fit her and her students. When she came to the next meeting, she said, "I tried it. I told one of the boys I didn't like the way he was treating me, that he'd hurt my feelings. The boy said, 'Good. I don't like the way you're treating me.'" We all responded how positive this was, that dialogue had begun!

CHRISTIE: You should go back later and talk with him when he's not being hostile or misbehaving. Catch him being good and reinforce it.

JAMES: This will resonate with him.

SUSAN: It will be slow.

MARI: He hasn't spoken to me like that since. He's not so hostile all the time.

CRYSTAL (first-year teacher; telling of a student who is a lot like this): One day I got exasperated with his yelling at me and I yelled at him. I said, "This is how you sound and it hurts my ears."

CHRISTIE: You have to keep trying and being flexible, trying new things but keeping in mind that this is a person who, for whatever reason, is stressed. [What she finds so hard about teaching, she says, is the total emotional stress.] Some days I totally revert to how I was taught.

CRYSTAL: One day when I totally freaked, I called a friend here at NYU. She said, "You're entitled."

The conversation continued with a discussion of their children's lives and the conditions in their schools and where the sources of support are for them. Mari was being told in many ways and at many levels that she was not alone.

When Mari returned to the group in September, she was working with a kindergarten class in the same school. She had no experience with such young children so she came to the conversation group for help and guidance, and she proceeded to come regularly throughout the year and serve as a mentor for new teachers experiencing difficult classes. She had used her last month of school with her fourth graders and her time with the kindergartners to learn to engage with her students. Like a zealous convert, she wanted to spread the good news.

For me, Mari's story is noteworthy not only for what it tells about the power of autobiography in shaping teachers' understandings and practice, but also for what it tells me about the limits on the ways of knowing our students that are possible in teacher education. I had advised Mari when she transferred into the program and continued to do so through her remaining 2 years. I had worked with her in classes. But I did not *know* her; nor did her peers in the program and the conversation group. Formal interactions between professor and student were not sufficient for Mari's story to emerge. Over time, all of us have learned that there have to be ways for the type of authentic conversation around real classroom issues that is the substance of the conversation group's discourse to emerge in preservice teacher education. We have also learned that groups like this are essential in the continuing professional development of teachers.

Recurring Patterns in Conversation

As I have studied our 4 years of conversation, I have identified six topics that occur with enough regularity to be considered critical foci for beginning teachers. These are assessment; classroom management; contexts and norms of schools; curriculum; getting, changing, and keeping a job; and children. Each of these is addressed within a framework of providing professional support and enabling self-knowledge that seems to characterize the interaction of the group. There is a cycle to these topics over a year. These are described in Figures 5.1, 5.2, and 5.3 where a year begins with the start of school in September.

Patterns of occurrence for these topics have to do with who initiates them and the cycle of activity in schools. Getting a job, for example, is a topic raised most often by preservice students in anticipation of December or May graduations (see Figure 5.1). Discussion of the contexts and norms of schools are interwoven with discussions of jobs in ways that suggest that the conditions of the workplace have a definite impact on new teachers' perceptions of teaching and on experienced teachers' considerations about their workplace. When teachers in the group find themselves in settings where there is virtually no support, the issue of finding a new job arises. This is as true of a first-year teacher as it is of teachers in their second and third years. Decisions about moving from one school to another seem to peak at points when teachers are most free to move: January and summer months (see Figure 5.1).

Discussions of classroom management originate with new teachers, particularly those who are struggling. They are never initiated by the preservice teachers in the group. Conversations about classroom management often are interwoven with discussions of problem children. These generally are initiated by teachers who are concerned about a child's progress and fit in the community of the classroom (Rust, 1999b). Like discussions of classroom management, these rarely are initiated by the preservice teachers, although they actively participate in discussions of both topics. Discussions of classroom management interweave with those about particular children. Both seem to follow the cycle of activities in schools, with classroom management appearing to be a nonissue in April, when city-wide tests are being given, and in summer, when teachers are not in classrooms (see Figure 5.2).

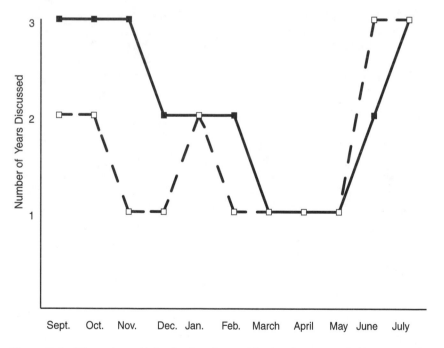

Figure 5.1. Discussion of jobs (broken line) and school norms (solid line) over three years.

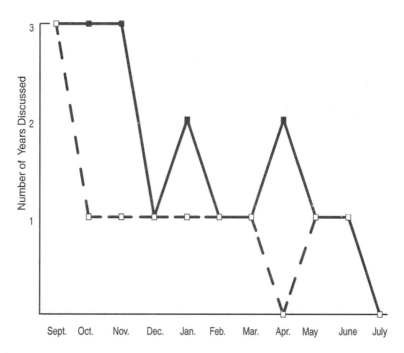

Figure 5.2. Discussion of classroom management (broken line) and kids (solid line) over three years.

Discussions of curriculum weave through discussions of assessment (see Figure 5.3). Both are, in fact, central foci of the group's conversation, occupying approximately 50% of our discussions. Curriculum surfaces in a variety of ways that relate to the cycle of activity in schools as well as to the group's interests and expertise. In January and February of the first year, participants organized meetings to focus exclusively on literacy. Everyone came with examples of what they do in their classrooms. Since then, discussions of curriculum have included such varied topics as balanced literacy, various math programs, science curricula, field trips, the implications of state and city standards for teaching, and curriculum imposed by the city on failing schools. Participants share materials with one another. They have even developed curriculum together. Assessment is woven into these conversations and assumes a critical focus for the group in November when new members of the group hold their first set of parent–teacher conferences. In recent years, the imposition of new city-wide tests in January has spurred discussion of assessment among the entire group.

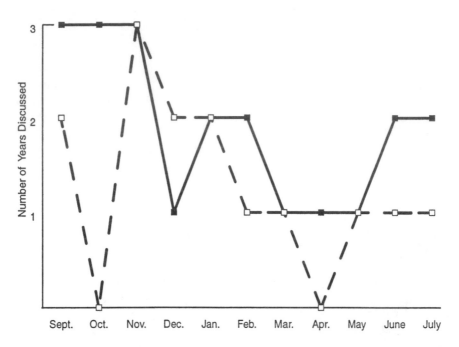

Figure 5.3. Discussion of curriculum (solid line) and assessment (broken line) over three years.

Over time, it has become clear that this predictable set of topics appear and disappear at regular points across the year in a conversational spiral. Each time a topic appears, it is handled with greater depth and sophistication, mirroring the experiential growth of the various members of the group. Thus, there is a development and rounding out of a topic across time and relative to experience. Preservice students address a topic in one way, first-year teachers in another, and second-year teachers in still another. Take, for example, the issue of classroom management. Preservice students talk about classroom management in general terms, as James, a senior at the time, does in the following excerpt: "There should always be a 'why,' a reason that teachers are asking children to behave in certain ways. If it's always the teacher's job to make sure children behave, then they never take responsibility for their behavior themselves."

First-year teachers, in contrast, speak about specific problems, often inviting advice, as Karen, who is teaching first grade, does in her first week of school: "Here's what I did, the sort of schedule I set for the first 3 days: overview of day, math, free writing, thinking, independent reading—they read out loud a lot. My hardest time is the last hour. We're on the rug too long. I've tried BINGO and other songs. I just don't know what else to do."

Second-year teachers talk about what they did or are doing as a way of providing guidance to the beginning teachers, as Robert, a second-year teacher, does in response to Karen:

> I have monolingual and dual lingual kids so I did some mixing. Starting in September is so different from starting in January [which is when he began teaching]. I audiotaped myself yesterday. I discovered that I was noticing the positive stuff, saying things like "congratulations to. . . ." Before I did the taping, I thought I was being too firm, maybe talking too much. I am working on a lot of community building. I'm doing things like Putups and developing routines. . . . Every day starts with a motivational song. It takes the first 10 minutes. Today, I started with "I Believe I Can Fly." . . . Twenty-nine is a different sound from 20, which is the number of students I had last year. I'm wondering if what I am hearing is a good sound.

This pattern has held throughout our 4 years of conversation to the extent that I now know that it will be first-year teachers who raise the issue of classroom management, and experienced teachers in the group who will address it; preservice teachers who worry about finding jobs, and experienced teachers who push one another to move to schools where they will have support to teach as they were taught to teach; experienced teachers who will raise the issues of curriculum and assessment, and preservice teachers who will take notes and probe for further information.

Developing Expertise

I now can track a similar pattern in individuals. For example, by looking at Christie's talk about classroom management as a preservice student, first-year teacher, and third-year teacher, one can see a pattern that parallels that of the group (see Table 5.1). As a preservice student, Christie talks in general terms, draws on her autobiography, and refers to what her cooperating teacher has done. A few months later as a first-year teacher, she fusses with various facets of classroom management. By the time the issue comes up again in her third year of teaching, she has worked through various problems, is offering advice, and is describing how she determines practice. There are no signs of ambivalence in this

Table 5.1. Christie's Discussions of Classroom Management over Four Years

Preservice (June)	First Year (November)	Third Year (September)
Claims her confidence comes from 8 years of summer camp working as and with an assistant. She has learned to set standards with assistants and with parents.	Uses mediation techniques: no interrupting, no name calling; tell me what happened; tell me how not to do it again; focuses on one person at a time; ignores the rest of the stuff.	She and her partner had a long conversation. Partner wanted to lay rules out. Christie said, "Make up rules as you go along."
Feels that children have to be trained to work in independent, responsible ways.	15 students that used to get all of her time, 15 that were ignored; now the latter get her attention and the others are ignored!	Was so exhausted in her first year. By January, hit a brick wall.
Tries various strategies that have been modeled by her cooperating teacher.	Switched from fines to noticing and acknowledging good behavior.	Says, "You'll reinvent a lot. The good thing is that they'll do a lot of what you ask."
Advocacy is central to her stance: "How do kids make sense of this?" Thinks the question "What did they say you did?" makes sense; she's seen it at work in transitions in her school.	Whispers a lot.	Asks, "Do you have a buddy?"
Cooperating teacher asks misbehaving child if he's okay. Implication is that child would not behave that way if he were all right.	Doesn't wait; gets started.	
	Decided in early Nov. to stop punishing kids for misbehavior. Really trying to make them feel like good kids. Kids shooting off caps in classroom (wonders to herself why she never saw cooperating teacher punishing for misbehavior).	
	Finds herself mean, berating kids. "I embarrass this one girl in my class" (child has no skills; an emotional cripple). I want a guidance counselor for me.	
	Says there are fist fights in the class at least once a week.	
	Tells of an awful trip to the park: Seven fist fights, burrs in hair. Next trip she ends up yelling at the kids about a tree branch.	

third year. She seems secure and confident to the point that she is able to hold her ground with her partner in an inclusion class.

What this pattern among individuals and the group suggests is the development of expertise. It shows a progression from a stance that is marked by generalities in talk and in preservice teachers' reported actions to a stance in teacher talk that is marked by confidence and intimate knowledge of children, classrooms, and schools. In the conversation group, the preservice teachers' inexperience often contrasts rather sharply with the intimate "shop talk" of the classroom teachers (even the first-year teachers) whose knowledge of and relationships with their students lead them into describing their students as "my kids" and gives their conversation a texture not present in the talk of preservice students (Rust, 1999b).

The talk of the preservice students places them in Berliner's (1988) category of novice teachers: Their talk is often "very rational, relatively inflexible, and tend[s] to conform to whatever rules and procedures [they] were told to follow" (p. 41). In Fuller and Bown's (1975) stage theory, they are at the survival stage. They are concerned about "adequacy and survival as a teacher, about class control, about being liked by pupils, about supervisors' opinions, about being observed, evaluated, praised, and failed" (p. 37). Berliner (1988) writes:

> The novice and the advanced beginner, though intensely involved in the learning process, may also lack a certain responsibility for their actions. This occurs because they are labeling and describing events, following rules, and recognizing and classifying contexts, but not actively determining through personal action what is happening. (p. 42)

The conversation of first-year teachers seems to show fairly quick movement from being what Berliner (1988) describes as novices and advanced beginners into becoming what he describes as competent teachers:

> They make conscious choices about [what] they are going to do. They set priorities and decide on plans. They have rational goals and choose sensible means for reaching the ends they have in mind. In addition, they can determine what is and what is not important—from their experience they know what to attend to and what to ignore. At this stage, teachers learn to make curriculum and instruction decisions. . . . Because they are more personally in control of the events around them, following their own plans, and responding only to the information that they choose to, teachers at this stage tend to feel more responsibility for what happens. They are not detached. Thus, they often feel emotional about success and failure in a way that is different and more intense than that of novices or advanced beginners. And they have more vivid memories of their successes and failures as well. (p. 42)

Following Berliner's taxonomy, the talk of some first-year teachers and most second- and third-year teachers in the group seems to give evidence of their moving into what Berliner describes as the proficient stage. This is the stage, writes Berliner,

> at which intuition and know-how become prominent. . . . At this stage, a teacher may notice without conscious effort that today's mathematics lesson is bogging down for the same reason that last week's spelling lesson bombed. At some higher level of categorization, the similarities between disparate events are understood. This holistic recognition of similarities allows the proficient individual to predict events more precisely, since he or she sees more things as alike and therefore as having been experienced before. . . . The proficient performer, however, while intuitive in pattern recognition and in ways of knowing, is still analytic and deliberative in deciding what to do. (pp. 42–43)

They are committed to teaching and are well on their ways to becoming the expert pedagogues that Berliner places at the zenith of the profession.

The movement of these new teachers from the novice stage to the proficient stage in a matter of a year or two of teaching may surprise some who, like Berliner (1996), hold that it takes 10 years for a novice to acquire the qualities of mind, the knowledge, and the rapid and skilled performance that we associate with expertise. Elsewhere (Rust, 1999b), I have described the swiftness of these new teachers' development and suggested that the supportive context of the conversation group, coupled with the fact of the members having graduated from the same program, may work together to facilitate a trusting atmosphere in which authentic conversation about teaching is possible. What I have not addressed until now is the interplay among individual development as evidenced in teacher talk, development of the group's conversation, and development of the group as a whole.

Conversation as Professional Development

Beth, a first-year teacher, came to a recent meeting of the conversation group for the first time this year. She is having a very difficult time in a suburban setting where she is working as a teaching assistant. Her job is to provide support for five boys who require special education services for learning disabilities. Hers is not an under-resourced school in which students, teachers, and administrators are working within narrowly pre-scribed curriculum mandates that permit little initiative from teachers to respond to children's needs (see Rust, 1999a). Yet Beth is struggling be-cause everything that she is being told to do with her students, and the ways in which they are being excluded from the mainstream work of the classroom, is working against her beliefs about equity and her knowledge of good teaching practice. Her students are not given extra time to complete assignments, although they need it. Beth is not allowed to adapt the curriculum into parts that are both meaningful and manageable for her students. She is not allowed to remove them from the class and teach them in ways that are most appropriate given their disabilities. Most troubling to her is the clear and unequivocal hostility that the classroom teacher directs toward Beth's students. After listening to her description of her setting, various members of the group, including me, urged her to leave at the December break and transfer to another teaching position. These were not idle suggestions. They were drawn from our collective experience of having worked in and witnessed members of the group in debilitating situations.

The suggestions that Beth move began slowly. Susan, my co-facilitator, told her of a job that was available immediately. She was rebuffed by Beth. Sandra and James both said that their experience told them there isn't much you can do if your philosophy of teaching is not shared by others in the school. Robert urged her to go. The three of them are in their third year of teaching. All are in new jobs and were basking in the pleasure of working in settings where their understandings of teaching and learning are honored and shared.

Throughout the evening, members of the group kept coming back to Beth's situation and urging her to move. This happened a half dozen times until James, who had suggested early on that she leave, turned to me and spoke again:

> "Frances, how long have we been coming here?"
>
> "Four years," I replied.
>
> James mused, "Four years! What I have learned from these meetings is when to leave. I've had four jobs in the 2½ years since I graduated. After being forced out of my first one abruptly, I went to work in a shelter for battered women. The sadness of it was overwhelming. Those kids deserved better and I wanted to do it, but I realized that in a given structure, you can only be so effective. If you're overwhelmed, the students must be twice as overwhelmed. You can't be effective in an environment like that. I realized that the reason I hadn't been coming [to the conversation group] was that I was so depressed. I left the job. A point came when I realized that I was almost repeating the pattern those kids were suffering. I was almost a tool of oppression. I was eating away at what I want to bring to this profession. Each year that I

feel this way, I have less to give. You don't want to be there just for a paycheck. I've learned that I have to wait until the moment comes when I'm staying there for me. That's the biggest gift you have to give a child."

Others followed. The conversation moved along. Other topics were raised, but the group continued to return to Beth, urging her to move. Nina, another first-year teacher who had graduated with Beth, said, "It pains me to see you like this. I am in a tough situation but I'm loving it. What I know how to do is valued. I am getting a lot of support." Beth pleaded that the five children with whom she works need her. Sandra told Beth about her 2-year experience in a setting where there was no support and no resources. She contrasted it with her current job:

> I was attached to my kids for 2 years. I had to leave because it was not good for me. Like James said, "If it's not good for me, it's not good for them." I used to take one day off once a month. Now, I don't want to miss a thing! I get up at 6 a.m., leave by 6:30, and practically run to school.

Finally, Susan suggested that Beth's hesitance might have to do with imagining other possibilities. Susan said, "It's hard to make that break and it's hard to imagine what it could be like in a different environment. You've heard what everyone has said; you need to simply make the break and have faith that it will be okay. You have to entertain the possibility that it can be better."

I offer this story because it illustrates remarkable development in our conversation as well as among the individuals in the group. This conversation simply could not have taken place 4 years earlier. We were too new to one another and to the work of teaching. While we knew one another 4 years ago, we knew one another as students and graduates of a particular teacher education program. Although the experienced teachers in the group shared their stories with us, we had not developed the capacity to hear stories that were about issues we had not yet confronted. "When to leave" had not been a part of our conversation as faculty and students. It is not something that is taught in teacher education; it is not appropriate to teach about leaving when our focus is rightly on beginning well. If thoughts about when to leave were on the minds of some of the experienced teachers in the group 4 years earlier, we, as a group of seniors and recent graduates, were not ready for it. Nor were we ready for the types of in-depth discussions of curriculum and norms of schools that now focus our attention. The group has developed. The conversation has expanded and, in the process, our ability to support and educate one another has developed too.

Over these 4 years, we have learned that professional development in teaching might best be accomplished as a peer-mediated experience. Clark (1999) suggests that

> movement toward expertise may be stimulated and supported by authentic, sustained professional contact, in context, with a teacher whose level of expertise is but slightly different than one's own, and who has recently completed the same teacher education program. In the language of social constructivism, two learners whose Zones of Proximal Development overlap may have more to offer one another than two whose Zones of Proximal Development are worlds or generations apart. In this formulation, expertise is seen as co-constructed and contextually situated rather than as a fixed body of knowledge and skill that can be somehow "passed on" from master to apprentice. (p. 6)

The development of our conversation over time has involved us as a group in breaking down the barriers between preservice and inservice teaching. My students now work with recent program graduates who are their cooperating teachers, and our graduates return each month to share their stories and draw on the wisdom of the group. And while we continually have new members join the group, our talk has moved from a general survey of the conditions of teaching and schools to a genuinely interactive discussion in which members draw on one another's knowledge and expertise. This is due in large measure to the continued participation of several members of the group since its inception; but it also relates to the development of our understandings about what the first years of teaching entail and what works in teacher preparation to support new teachers' transition to the real world of schools.

There is a complex interplay of individual and collective storytelling in our ongoing conversation that resides in trust and confidence in one another. This interplay, it seems to me, has worked in ways that promote the development of the various participants as well as the whole group. The conversation group is, we have concluded, a form of sustainable professional development for teachers and by teachers that is not a substitute for teacher education. Rather, it enables a contextualized and selective revisitation of ideas and activities first encountered when members were student teachers. And beyond the revisitation of ideas and concepts from preservice days, the more experienced teachers' stories and advice break new ground and constitute a credible curriculum of professional development for new teachers in challenging circumstances. In our conversation group meetings, we gather around the table and talk with one another in ways that blur the distinctions between preservice and inservice teaching and that move us forward in pursuit of teaching well.

MENTORS' CONVERSATIONS ABOUT MENTORING

What do novices and experienced mentors talk about? Like new teachers, they talk about themselves and their work. Over a period of 2 academic years (2 semesters per year, October–January and March–June), I (Lily) had the privilege of working with a group of mentors in the course entitled "Mentoring Skills and Practices." The course met weekly for 2 hours. Course sessions focused on furthering the mentors' understandings about the practice of mentoring as related to recent theorizing and research in the area, as well as to their particular contexts of practice. All of the course participants were experienced secondary teachers working in a variety of curriculum areas. Some were new to the role of mentor. Others were experienced mentors. They came from both the Arab and Jewish sectors of Israel. Their purpose was to improve their practice and thereby the teaching and learning experiences of their mentees and their students.

Every other week, our sessions took the form of "learning conversations" in which we focused on the writing and sharing of mentors' stories and cases from the field. During these sessions the mentors shared their experiences, dilemmas, conflicts, and stories of success and failure with the group. I (who had been a mentor for many years) functioned both as mediator and meta-mentor. I adopted the role of co-thinker (Feiman-Nemser & Parker, 1994) by encouraging the mentors to articulate their beliefs about mentoring and to reflect on how these were translated into action in their work as mentors (Schön, 1983). As a meta-mentor, I tried to articulate the strategies that I adopted as mediator during the conversations so as to model a reflective approach to mentoring, which they might then transfer to their own interactions with teachers.

Five months after the termination of the course, I began my analysis of these conversations, which had been tape recorded and transcribed. In addition, I maintained a reflective journal that enabled me to record the insights I was gaining as a result of my interaction with the mentors. These were substantiated by field notes taken in each of the meetings. As I read through the data, I could picture the sessions very vividly. I was transported back to room number 617, where the sessions were held. It is a relatively small room with table-chairs organized in a semicircle to encourage interaction among participants and to break the frontal mode of university teaching. As so often happens, the seats that participants chose on the first day of class remained theirs throughout much of the course. In the first year, three female novice mentors from the Jewish sector, Tali, Adina, and Rina, sat together at the left-hand side of the room. Opposite them, five mentors from the Arab sector (all men) sat in one block, with two novice mentors, Jamal and Yanir, like bookends on either side of three experienced mentors, Habed, Salim, and Taufik. The space between these two groups was filled by mentors from the Jewish sector: two men, Avi and David, and four women, Irit, Rutie, Dita, and Yehudit. I remember trying to learn their names according to the "block" they assigned themselves to in the room. Only toward the end of the first year did participants begin to change places and to mingle. By the end of the second year, they had abandoned their fixed seating; they had become a more homogeneous group of peers, functioning in an atmosphere of trust and solidarity.

How had the group coalesced? Did the conversational nature of the sessions play a role in bringing the group together? Did the structure of the course function as a framework for articulating and developing understandings about practice? As I analyzed our 2 years of conversation, I was able to track our evolution from a group of individuals to a community of professionals by focusing on three major conversational themes: identity, voice, and community.

Establishing Identity as a Mentor

Differences in the talk of new and experienced mentors' perspectives parallel those between new and experienced teachers at NYU. The new mentors' talk at the beginning of the course was suggestive of Berliner's (1988) novice stage in that it was marked by general concerns about accountability. These concerns were voiced very rationally, in a relatively inflexible manner, and showed that the new mentors were trying to conform to whatever rules or procedures they were told to follow. In contrast, the experienced mentors' responses were marked by sensitivity to local needs and recognition of the importance of adopting a flexible approach. The experienced mentors' stance is compatible with what Berliner (1988) defines as the state of becoming a competent teacher: "They can determine what is and what is not important . . . are more personally in control of events, and [are] not detached" (p. 42). Such differences were particularly evident in the early days of the course and are exemplified in the following discussion between Tali, a novice mentor of teachers of computer science, and two experienced mentors, Dita and Yehudit:

> TALI: My problem is that, on the one hand, the inspector expects me to convince teachers about the assets of computer assisted learning, but how can I even start talking about teaching through computers when teachers are not really into learning

the basic technicalities of using a computer? I mean, on the one hand, the system pushes for introducing computers in schools and, on the other hand, teachers' minds are on other issues, such as coping with teaching large and heterogeneous classes. So one thing is the desired and the other is the reality of situation and I kind of feel that I am not fulfilling my role.

DITA: You mean you are not fulfilling your role in terms of the demands of the system. I mean what you are expected to do by the inspectors who hired you, but what about the real needs of teachers? That is more important. I think you have to be flexible.

YEHUDIT: I agree with Dita. You are thinking only in terms of what you think you are expected to do from above. In my case, for example, I am also a mentor for computers. I have been doing this for 7 years already and I have learned that one thing is what the system expects from you and another is what the teachers expect from you as their mentor. Sometimes you have to realize that what comes from above is just not realistic, and the constraints of the school system will inevitably push you to become more of a technician and SOS kit to the teachers. You just have to become like a *mechaba srefot* [Hebrew for "putting out the fire," meaning solving problems on the spot] and forget all about doing the right kind of mentoring.

TALI: That's all very nice, but then it is the inspector who will decide whether to hire me or not next year. I mean I still have to show some evidence that I am succeeding at what I am being paid for!

What is fascinating in this exchange is the seeming indifference of the experienced mentors to the concerns of the new mentor. Clearly, at this point in the group's history, the experienced mentors were not seeing themselves as mentors to the novice in the group, and Tali did not seem to be anticipating that they would help her. As I reflected on this exchange, I attributed Tali's focus on accountability to those who hired her to her stance as a novice and to being at that stage in her career that Fuller and Brown (1975) describe as survival. She was concerned primarily "about her supervisor's opinions, about being observed, evaluated, praised and failed" (p. 37). At this point in her professional development, I reasoned, she was not ready to listen to other voices, particularly ones with destabilizing messages.

Experience, however, was not the only factor that seems to have shaped mentors' conversation and particularly their level of concern about their role in "the system." Among mentors from the Jewish sector, whether experienced or new, accountability to the system was a major conversational focus at the beginning of the first year. This finding intrigued me. I wondered if there was a difference in the schools and contexts in which these mentors were working, since the topic of accountability to the system did not seem to be an area of concern for the experienced Arab mentors in the group. Jamal's reply to Yehudit and Tali in the conversation cited above provides an example:

JAMAL: I don't understand why you have such a problem. With us it's simpler. Everybody knows that if I visit a teacher, it is because the inspector has asked me to and that there are certain things that the teachers will have to be willing to do and try out.

YEHUDIT (interrupts): That's because in your sector the mentor is seen more like an inspector so the teachers will probably not tell you what they really think.

JAMAL (laughing): Maybe not, but it makes things less complicated for me. I don't have this conflict about who I represent.

My first reaction to Jamal was that he was oversimplifying the situation. However, as the issue of accountability was further elaborated in the conversations, I began to see that whereas the mentors working in the Jewish sector tended to see themselves experiencing conflict between their expected roles and their realized roles in the field, the Arab mentors felt no such role conflict. They attributed this to the highly prestigious status of the mentor in the Arab sector, as compared with the ambiguous and vaguely defined status of the mentor in the Jewish sector. Habed, one of the Arab mentors, and Avi, one of the Jewish mentors, stressed this last point in response to Yehudit:

HABED: I think Yehudit is right. It's because the teachers see us in the Arab schools like inspectors. Even the principal of the school treats us as kind of semi-inspectors.

AVI: We, in the Jewish schools, are neither inspectors nor teachers. We are some kind of mutation, something in between a teacher, an inspector, and a counselor.

McIntyre and Hagger (1996) assert that the widespread use of the term *mentor* is possible only because of a general lack of clarity about its meaning. They suggest that there is a need to elaborate and refine a generic concept of mentoring that would distinguish it from other roles and relationships in the system. Mentors from the Jewish sector did not experience such clarity, resulting in their preoccupation with establishing the parameters of the mentor's role and their concern about accountability to the system.

Establishing the Mentor's Voice

Reflecting on the experienced mentors' seeming indifference to Tali's concerns about defining her role, I noted that at the beginning of the course, it seemed as if the conversations mainly served the purpose of making oneself heard. The metaphor that comes to mind is a series of auditions. The mentors' contributions to the conversations took the form of short monologues that provided a physical space and a stage—a kind of sounding board—that the mentors often had complained was lacking in their daily practice outside the university. The mentors did not yet know one another. Thus, they seemed concerned about establishing their voice, their perspectives. They were not yet engaged in conversation.

As the course progressed, there was less focus on providing a platform for voicing complaints about the system. As participants became more receptive to each other, they began to talk with rather than at each other, and the conversation became richer, providing a forum for more in-depth exploration of the unique voices that the mentors were developing.

Toward the middle of the second year of conversations, I noticed that the novice mentors in the group were developing a more critical stance toward the impact of systemic factors on their mentoring interactions. In particular, they spoke about how accountability to the system can become either an asset or a liability to the mentor's intervention. In the following conversation between two novice mentors, Rina is sharing parts of a journal entry with the group. She is talking about her learning as a novice mentor during the year:

> RINA: When I look back, I think I was so uptight about certain goals that I thought I was supposed to fulfill. Now I look at things differently. I can see more of me in the whole setup, and I understand how one does not work in isolation with those goals. I mean these goals are constantly revised and changed as the situation demands, and I have become aware that I need to kind of navigate according to where the teachers are. It's choosing what glasses suit me and then deciding which ones to wear for the specific situation.

YANIR: I can identify with Rina in that I am now convinced that you cannot follow one agenda all the time. I mean it is not realistic. With the teachers I work with, I find myself changing strategies and goals all the time, and I think I have at last found a way to get to them that I also feel comfortable with. I mean that works for me also.

Rina's and Yanir's comments illustrate the ways in which the novice mentors in the group were developing their own voices. The search for her voice within the system was particularly evident in Rina's choice of the phrase "suit me" when referring to which pair of glasses she would choose to wear for a specific mentoring interaction. Yanir's agreement, signaled in his choice of the phrase "that works for me also," conveys the understandings that he has gained about himself as a mentor and about the role in general. In a way, Rina and Yanir are saying not only that they are finding their voices but also that they are positioning themselves in relation to other voices in the larger discourse of mentoring. They are acknowledging what research on mentoring makes clear: Mentors' roles and mentoring practices are shaped, to a great extent, by programmatic, administrative, and organizational aspects of schools and school systems, and by the ways in which other roles such as teacher, principal, and inspector are defined in the system (Booth, 1995; Cameron & O'Hara, 1997; Carmin, 1988; Daloz, 1986; Elliot & Calderhead, 1995; Gehrke, 1988; Kram, 1986; Maynard & Furlong, 1993; McIntyre & Hagger, 1996; Zey, 1984).

Experienced mentors, too, talked about having become less preoccupied with the system. In contrast with the novice mentors in the group, though, they seemed to go beyond expressing a need to identify a voice of their own to becoming more articulate in talking about the impact of their personal dispositions and styles on the quality of mentoring relationships. While the novice mentors' talk developed from concerns about replicating in their practice the voices of their inspectors to beginning to identify their own voices, the experienced mentors' talk developed from an initial concern about being connected to the needs of teachers to identifying and addressing the uniqueness of their voices and reflecting on the beliefs and patterns of behavior that characterized them as individuals in the system. A conversation among three experienced mentors, Irit, Habed, and Dita, in the session just cited illustrates this shift:

DITA (reading to the group from her journal): I have become aware that there are three selves in me that come to play when I am mentoring. One is the personal self, what I bring with me as Dita, the person, with all my history as a new immigrant in this country Israel and as a woman. The other Dita is the professional with my academic and teaching background. The third self has to do with my ideologies and ideas about education. These three present themselves in every mentoring interaction. I think what I have learned here is to become conscious of how these affect what I say, how I listen, how I respond, and how it might affect the mentee. It is something that was in me all the time but it was more intuitive.

HABED: I have begun to think more and more about the gap between how I define my role and what I actually do in the field. It is something we spoke about at the beginning of the course and was less of a problem for me then, but now I kind of realize that functioning like an inspector in the field probably has certain consequences for how the mentees interpret what I say or what I suggest to them. This is really not how I would like them to interpret what I say.

IRIT: Like Dita, I feel I am becoming more and more preoccupied with defining for myself who I am as Irit the mentor and how I am seen by the system, and whether the people see the uniqueness in me, Irit, as compared to other mentors. I mean I can now see that I "sound" different from other mentors and I kind of like that.

Dita's allusion to three selves that present themselves simultaneously in her mentoring is reminiscent of Day's (1998) portrayal of the different selves of a teacher that operate as competing images in the act of teaching. According to Day, these are the *educative self*, the *ideological* or *emancipatory self*, and the *personal self*. Dita's naming these three selves suggests both how closely allied the work of teaching and mentoring are and how extremely difficult it is to separate the two roles. Further, the quality of reflection evident in this exchange among three experienced mentors suggests a remarkable and subtle transformation in the group that establishes them as reflective practitioners (Schön, 1983) who are engaged in the articulation of emergent gaps between their espoused theories and their actions.

As the mentors entered more deeply into the conversation, they began to raise dilemmas related to distinguishing their selves-as-teachers from their selves-as-mentors. The following excerpt from the conversation of Rutie, a novice mentor, at the beginning of the second year provides an example:

Since I began working as a mentor for computers last year, I have a feeling that I am being drawn by the teachers into functioning for them as a teacher more than as a mentor. I mean I see mentoring as supporting the teacher in her ongoing work and I see teaching as supporting the pupil. But with me, for some reason which I would like to clarify here, it seems that I cannot distinguish between my behavior as a teacher from my behavior as a mentor when I am doing mentoring. I allow the teachers to manipulate me into helping the children with their computers. As I think about it, it may be that it's more comfortable for me that way, to do teaching, because that's what I know best, having worked with children for so many years. I keep asking myself is it because I am easily inclined towards working with pupils rather than with teachers that I function more as a teacher than as a mentor when I do mentoring?

Mentoring, as McIntyre and Hagger (1996) note, is not a "zero level" activity devoid of teaching expertise and of the difficulty of disentangling one practice from the other. Rutie's comments make this clear. The feeling of role conflict that Rutie expressed also was addressed by Adina, another novice mentor:

I identify with you so much! I have this constant conflict of trying to sort out for myself how my teaching affects my mentoring, especially when the teachers want to hear tips from the field and I give it to them using my teaching as an example. But I have come to realize that more than what my teaching does to my mentoring, I feel that being a mentor has affected my teaching. I have become more tuned in to the individual pupil, more of a counselor in my own teaching.

Adina's comment was followed by Tali's account of an incident as a mentor of student teachers that clarified for her the duality of roles that she experienced at the beginning of her work as a mentor. The incident also prompted her to reflect on the roles that she was espousing as a mentor:

I was talking to the mentees about theories of learning when suddenly one of the teachers asked me: "This is all very nice but how do you as a teacher apply this in your own teaching?" At that moment, I realized that I was neglecting the teacher in me almost completely, because now that I reflect on the incident, I realize that I did not want to reveal the teacher in me. I wanted to be regarded closer to a university lecturer, probably because I had had enough of the teacher's image shadowing me and here was my chance to "exhibit a new self."

The conflict of disentangling one role from the other was a recurrent conversational topic among the novices throughout the course. As I examined the development of this theme, I noticed that there was a marked change in their discourse on this topic over the 2 years: At the beginning, there was an expressed need on the part of the novices to arrive at clear-cut boundaries that distinguished one role from the other; toward the second year, their conversations conveyed new understandings of how their role as mentors had an impact on their teaching and how the two roles often operated in complementary ways. I interpreted this shift as a sign that the novice mentors were arriving at reconciliation between the two roles. I also saw it as a sign of their professional growth into learning to become more tolerant of ambiguity.

Two weeks after the conversation between Adina and Tali, I asked the group to think about the issue of teaching and mentoring and to reflect on how these two roles presented themselves in their work. Because the experienced mentors initially did not voice conflicts related to "the teacher in them," I was surprised by their responses to my request. These suggest to me that, despite their silence, the experienced mentors had been thinking about this issue. Consider the following excerpt from the conversation 2 weeks later:

IRIT: What Rutie and Adina said last week about being a mentor and being a teacher made me think that for me it's like a continuation of being a good teacher. I mean, being a good mentor. The same impetus that sustains us as teachers sustains us as mentors at this later stage.

DITA: I thought to myself: The same way I am a good counselor to children I can be a good mentor. For me these two roles complement each other.

LILY: So you are both saying that if you are a good teacher then you can become a good mentor?

DITA: Not necessarily, although I think that a "bad" teacher cannot be a good mentor. But in order to be a good mentor you need additional skills.

YEHUDIT: I think that the skills that are essential for mentoring are communication skills—knowing to listen and to ask the appropriate questions that would encourage teachers to reflect.

AVI: Yes, but you also need that in teaching. For me, it is the difference between working with adults and working with children. With adults you are more of a colleague.

TAUFIK: I think that the difference is that in mentoring you need to develop skills that will help you to talk about someone's teaching.

IRIT: I agree with Taufik. It's learning about process, and about analyzing teaching.

A little later:

YEHUDIT: Rutie's story made me think about whether I was taking for granted the split that I make when I am teaching or mentoring. I find myself many times behaving like a teacher with the mentees. I kind of use a teacher-talk language, especially in workshops.

IRIT: I can empathize with that. The question–answer mode which we are so critical about when we teach and we do the same with the teachers, but with me it's less felt because I work mostly on a one to one in front of the computer.

In earlier work (Orland, 1997), I note the importance of what Bornstein and Bruner (1989) describe as asymmetrical conversations. These are conversations in which the themes that preoccupy one group become a trigger for the other group to pursue important issues. The exchange cited above seems to be an example of such asymmetrical conversation. Because the discussion was conducted mainly among the experienced mentors in the group, it made me think that probably the novice mentors' earlier discussions of dilemmas about role had served as a trigger for the experienced mentors to problematize an issue that, had it not been raised by the novices, might have remained unattended. The conversation of the novices had provided an important opportunity for the experienced mentors to reexamine aspects of their role that until then they probably had regarded as obvious, familiar, and resolved. Thus, the heterogeneity of the group actually challenged each party to examine and question tacit aspects of their practice.

Furthermore, the introduction of this issue by the novices and its follow-up by the experienced mentors made me think about ways in which understandings about teaching and mentoring were co-constructed among the members of the group over time as the mentors related to each other and as the conversation itself developed. In particular, I noticed how, from an initial view of mentoring as a natural continuation of teaching, the conversation developed into a reconsideration and elaboration of the distinctive skills that the participants saw as particular to the practice of mentoring.

Developing a Community of Learners

Taking a social theory perspective, Westheimer (1992) offers five common features that identify a community: shared beliefs, interaction and participation, interdependence, concern for individual and minority views, and meaningful relationships. Analyzing the development of our conversation over time, I found that toward the end of the second year, the group was growing into a community of learners. The mentors were developing a set of common understandings about the dualities implicit in the mentoring role. They were coming to our every-other-week meetings having reflected on prior conversations and they drew on their shared history together in the course to challenge and support one another. They were developing their own unique culture—what Hargreaves (1996) defines as "the way we do things around here," and the ways in which relations between teachers are articulated.

As a group, the mentors had begun to develop a shared terminology—a common language. I noticed, for example, that there were fewer exchanges conducted in a question–answer mode and more supportive and challenging talk like that which Florio-Ruane and Clark (1993) describe as authentic conversation. Phrases such as "I can identify/empathize with what you are saying," "tell me what you mean," and "this is our meeting point," had become commonly used patterns of interaction.

There was a commensurate shift in storytelling habits. Initially, most of the novice mentors' stories were told in the first person. They took little account of the mentoring context. As the course progressed, the novices' stories began to integrate more "voices." We heard about the teachers involved, the pupils, and even the administrators. Drawing on my earlier work, which focused on two novice mentors (Orland, forthcoming), I read this change as a sign that they had gained a more integrative understanding of the external and internal factors that affect mentoring interactions.

The experienced mentors' stories took a different developmental route. Initially, most of their stories were told from the point of view of their mentees and of other people in the system. They rarely spoke of their personal dilemmas or of role conflicts. As the course developed, their stories changed. They moved to attending to their own voice or adding a first-person dimension. I attributed these developmental changes to several factors: First, the reciprocal nature of the conversations prompted both novices and experienced mentors to attend to additional dimensions in their stories; second, my interventions during the conversations challenged the mentors to address aspects of their stories that had remained untold; and third, as a result of the developmental passages that both novices and experienced mentors had undergone throughout the 2 years of the course, the novices in the group learned to become more sensitive to personal and interpersonal factors influencing their interactions, and the experienced mentors began to think introspectively about their selves-as-mentors.

The following excerpt illustrates a reflective conversation around clarifying roles. Notice how, as the participants try to make themselves understood, they manage to construe new understandings of their role and to become aware of differences and similarities among members of the group as teachers and mentors. Notice also my questions and comments aimed at encouraging them to reflect on what they were learning about being a mentor from each other and on the potential benefits of conversational frameworks.

> IRIT: Rutie, you are putting emphasis on self-discovery, and Yehudit, on working on *tachles* [being down to earth].
> YEHUDIT: No, I work on person and product: the power that emerges from the teacher herself.
> IRIT: I work on process, discovering one's own potential. The final product for me is when the teacher finds in herself all the alternatives.
> YEHUDIT: But we expose the alternatives more technically, more specifically.
> IRIT: My work is not devoid of *tachles* because in my way there is also *tachlitiut* [being down to earth] but we connect it to something within the teacher.
> RUTIE: In each of you, there are products, but what led you to these products is different in every case.
> IRIT: That's true. The road is different but the goal is the same in that the teacher will want to continue teaching and survive in a creative manner.
> DITA: That's the difference between a counselor and teacher. A pupil who comes to me for counseling, I will give him the inner strength to cope. I will try to see where he is stuck.
> YEHUDIT: I will also work as a teacher on where the pupil is stuck, what he needs.
> DITA: So this is our meeting point.

LILY: Rutie, what did you learn about your mentoring from this
    conversation?
RUTIE: That I give a lot of credit to the teacher's potential.
LILY: Did the other people's reactions help you to focus?
RUTIE: It surfaced for me the process that I go through with my-
    self.
LILY: And Yehudit, what did you learn from Rutie about your
    mentoring?
YEHUDIT: I knew she works like this. But she doesn't know how I
    work. She thinks that I give recipes, but first I try to get to the
    inner truth of the teacher. I will see what her *emda* [stance] is
    without the recipes. Here I depart from Rutie. She gives credit
    to the teacher that she will come up with the answers by her-
    self. I say there are certain things that the teacher doesn't
    know so I suggest these things to the teacher and give her
    tips.
LILY: It seems that you were trying to understand the differences
    between the two of you and in the process also found some
    similarities. Through the conversation you were able to make
    sense of each other, and explain yourself to the other. That
    seems to be the narrative of this group.

The reflective conversations conducted throughout the course were
dominated by the voices of the Jewish women mentors. The men in the
group and the experienced mentors from the Arab sector seemed reluctant
to take part in conversations of this kind. In particular, I noticed that their
voice was more salient during those sessions that focused on cases that
I selected from the research literature on mentoring. I attributed this
tendency to issues of cultural background and to the fact that they were
all male mentors, which may have been a factor making them less inclined
to reveal feelings or hesitancies. It seems that despite the growth of shared
understandings during the course, there were some hurdles that we could
not surmount.

Still, Dita's questions to the group, after having shared with them a
traumatic incident in mentoring, is particularly illustrative of the culture
of talk that was emerging in the group in the final year. She asked the
mentors to relate to her story through three questions: What did my
actions reveal about myself? What would you have done instead? and
How did my actions reflect what you know about me? Her line of questioning suggests not only her growing confidence in herself but also her trust
of the group to help her solve the concrete problem and to help her
understand herself better. And it demonstrates a tacit recognition of the

ways in which the group had coalesced around professional discourse related to practice.

CONCLUSION

Throughout the chapter, we have been shaping a theory about the way conversations change and deepen among beginners in the field of teaching, between beginners and experienced teachers, and among experienced teachers and mentors. Our theory suggests that development of conversation and of individuals in sustained conversation over time is not a linear process. That both group and individual conversations became richer, more elaborate, and increasingly sophisticated is clear; however, our theory suggests to us that development of conversation and of individuals and groups in conversation over time is a recursive process in which there is a deepening of meaning and a broadening of understandings. As familiar topics like curriculum among the new teachers or agency among the mentors recur, they are addressed through the lens of the group's prior conversation. When new topics like "when to leave" appear, they, too, draw on the group's experience together. And when individuals approach a new task, they inevitably retrace the steps taken in the mastery of earlier tasks. Thus, new teachers must learn again how to enter school, and new mentors must remember how to begin teaching. Each comes to this new place with the experience of having begun before. What conversation seems to make possible is the capacity to draw not only on one's own memories but also on the collective memory of the group, thus enabling smoother beginnings and more thoughtful transitions between old and new roles. Time is essential for this process of development. So, too, is continuity.

In Frances Rust's group of preservice and inservice teachers, there are some members besides Rust and Haver who have been with the group since it began 4 years ago, and there are others who have joined since then who come on a regular basis. The fact of their continuance works in three ways to support the group's development. First, it enables new members to be easily drawn into the group's story of learning to teach because there is presumed to be a shared experiential base, which is the teacher education program. Second, it establishes breadth and texture in the conversation that allow participants, both new and experienced, to enter the story of learning to teach able to hear and draw from it in ways that were not available to us when we began. Third, this continuity of individuals over time also makes possible a community of teacher-learners whose stories weave together in ways that allow participants not only to encounter the complexity of teaching but also to see their personal narratives in the context of the broader narrative of learning to teach.

In Lily Orland's group, the various developmental shifts in the mentors' talk are important in that they point to the impact of interventions (in her case, a course structured around stories and cases) on the professional development of the participants. Moreover, integrating the sharing of stories in conversation as part of a formal academic course at the master's level proved to be an extremely successful and important educational experience for all concerned. It facilitated movement into an integrated understanding of teaching and mentoring for both novice and experienced mentors. Among the various activities of the mentoring course, the conversations were most powerful in helping to shape a professional framework for the mentors to safely reflect and articulate their assumptions about teaching, learning, and mentoring. Most of all, the conversations enabled the participants to explain themselves to others and, in the process, to clarify their own biases, tendencies, and inherent teaching styles.

Together, both the New Teachers' Conversation Group and the master's course for mentors provide substantial evidential support for Clark's (1995) claim that creating and sustaining conversational frameworks is a powerful tool for cultivating thoughtful teaching and mentoring:

> Authentic conversation, with its embedded personal stories, is a powerful yet challenging way to make sense of experience; to remember, reinterpret, and reorganize personal and social knowledge; to give and receive the support we all need to sustain ourselves and pursue our own visions and ideals. (p. 142)

The development of conversation, we conclude, resides in the participants, in their ability to focus together on important issues, in their willingness to come together regularly over time, and in their trust in the process itself. We see that the development of conversation is layered: There is development among individuals as they learn and grow in what becomes a company of friends; there is development of the group as it coheres over time; and there is development of conversation itself as the group's experience with an issue is elaborated in each new iteration. What begins as individual narrative becomes a shared conversation that blurs the arbitrary distinction between preservice teacher preparation and continuing professional development of teachers.

NOTE

The names of participants in both the New Teachers' Conversation Group and the mentoring course have been changed.

REFERENCES

Berliner, D. C. (1988). Implications of studies of expertise in pedagogy for teacher education and evaluation. In *New directions for teacher assessment. Proceedings of the 1988 ETS Invitational Conference* (pp. 39–67). Princeton, NJ: Educational Testing Service.

Berliner, D. C. (1996, November). Expertise in teaching. Keynote address to the Conference on Teaching and Teacher Education, Texas A & M University, College Station.

Booth, M. (1995). The effectiveness and role of the mentor in school: The student's view. In T. Kerry & A. S. Mayes (Eds.), *Issues in mentoring* (pp. 89–99). London: Routledge and Open University.

Bornstein, M., & Bruner, J. (1989). *Interaction in human development.* New York: New York University Press.

Bruner, J. (1990). *Acts of meaning.* Cambridge, MA: Harvard University Press.

Cameron, M., & O'Hara, P. (1997). Support and challenge in teacher education. *British Educational Journal, 23*(1), 15–25.

Carmin, C. (1988). The term mentor: A review of the literature and a pragmatic suggestion. *International Journal of Mentoring, 2*(2), 9–13.

Clark, C. M. (1995). *Thoughtful teaching.* New York: Teachers College Press.

Clark, C. M. (1999, July). *Cultivating expertise in teaching.* Paper presented to the International Study Association on Teachers and Teaching, Dublin, Ireland.

Connelly, F. M., & Clandinin, D. J. (1995). Narrative and education. *Teachers and Teaching: Theory and Practice, 1*(1), 73–85.

Daloz, L. (1986). *Effective teaching and mentoring.* San Francisco: Jossey-Bass.

Day, C. (1998). Working with the different selves of teachers: Beyond comfortable collaboration. *Educational Action Research, 6*(2), 255–273.

Elbaz, F. (in press). Writing as inquiry—Storying the teaching self in writing workshops. *Curriculum Inquiry.*

Elliot, B., & Calderhead, J. (1995). Mentoring for teacher development: Possibilities and caveats. In T. Kerry & A. S. Mayes (Eds.), *Issues in mentoring* (pp. 35–59). London: Routledge and Open University.

Feiman-Nemser, S., & Parker, M. B. (1994). Mentoring in context: A comparison of two U.S. programs for beginning teachers. *International Journal of Educational Research, 19*(8), 699–718.

Florio-Ruane, S. (1991). Conversation and narrative in collaborative research: An ethnography of the Written Literacy Forum. In C. Witherell & N. Noddings (Eds.), *Stories lives tell: Narrative and dialogue in education* (pp. 207–233). New York: Teachers College Press.

Florio-Ruane, S., & Clark, C. M. (1993, August). *Authentic conversation: A medium for research on teachers' knowledge and a context for professional development.* Paper presented to the International Study Association on Teacher Thinking, Goteborg, Sweden.

Fuller, F., & Bown, O. (1975). Becoming a teacher. In K. Ryan (Ed.), *Teacher education: Seventy-fourth Yearbook of the National Society for the Study of Educa-tion* (Part 2, pp. 35–37). Chicago: University of Chicago Press.

Gehrke, N. J. (1988). On preserving the essence of mentoring as one form of teacher leadership. *Journal of Teacher Education, 39*(1), 43–45.

Glaser, B. G., & Strauss, A. L. (1967). *The discovery of grounded theory: Strategies for qualitative research.* Chicago: Aldine.

Gomez, M., & Tabachnick, R. (1992). Telling teaching stories. *Teaching Education, 4*(2), 129–138.

Gudmundsdottir, S. (1997). Introduction to the theme issue of "narrative perspec-tives on research on teaching and teacher education." *Teaching and Teacher Education, 13*(1), 1–3.

Hargreaves, A. (1996). Cultures of teaching: A focus for change. In A. Hargreaves & M. G. Fullan (Eds.), *Understanding teacher development* (pp. 216–240). New York: Teachers College Press.

Kelchtermans, G. (1993). Getting the story, understanding the lives: From career stories to teachers' professional development. *Teaching and Teacher Education, 9*(5/6), 443–456.

Kram, K. E. (1986). *Mentoring at work: Developmental relationships in organizational life.* Glenview, IL: Scott, Foreman.

Maynard, T., & Furlong, J. (1993). Learning to teach and models of mentoring. In D. McIntyre, H. Hagger, & M. Wilkin (Eds.), *Mentoring: Perspectives on school-based teacher education* (pp. 69–85). London: Kegan.

McIntyre, D., & Hagger, H. (1996). Mentoring: Challenges for the future. In D. McIntyre & H. Hagger (Eds.), *Mentors in schools,* (pp. 144–165). London: David Fulton.

Orland, L. (1997). *Becoming a mentor: A study of the learning of novice mentors.* Unpublished doctoral dissertation, University of Haifa, Faculty of Education.

Orland, L. (forthcoming). Reading a mentoring situation: One aspect of learning to mentor. *Teaching and Teacher Education.*

Rust, F. O'C. (1999a, April). "I will not give in to this failure": New teachers at work in under-resourced schools. Paper presented at the annual meeting of the American Educational Research Association, Montreal.

Rust, F. O'C. (1999b). Professional conversations: New teachers explore teaching through conversation, story, and narrative. *Teaching and Teacher Education, 15*(4), 367–380.

Schön, D. A. (1983). *The reflective practitioner: How professionals think in action.* New York: Basic Books.

Schubert, W. (1991). Teacher lore: A basis for understanding praxis. In C. Wither-ell & N. Noddings (Eds.), *Stories lives tell: Narrative and dialogue in education* (pp. 207–233). New York: Teachers College Press.

Strauss, A., & Corbin, J. (1990). *Basics of qualitative research: Grounded theory proce-dures and techniques.* Newbury Park, CA: Sage.

Van Manen, M. (1990). *Researching lived experience.* Buffalo: State University of New York Press.

Westheimer, J. (1992, February). Communities and consequences: An inquiry into ideology and practice in teachers' professional work. *Educational Administration Quarterly, 35*(1), 71–105.

Witherell, C., & Noddings, N. (Eds.). (1991). *Stories lives tell: Narrative and dialogue in education.* New York: Teachers College Press.

Zey, M. G. (1984). *The mentor connection: Strategic alliances in corporate life.* New Brunswick & London: Transaction Publishers.

CHAPTER 6

Heroes of Our Own Tales: Presentation of Self in Conversation and Story

Stephen A. Swidler

T HE TALK IN AND OF professional and development and inquiry groups is shot through with, and perhaps primarily composed of, the telling of personal experience narratives, as this book attests. While the narrative voice is readily accessible and acceptable for the representation of teaching experience in these groups, it is not without its own difficulties and challenges to both narrator and audience. Among these challenges is a narrator's task of representing himself/herself in a story as the main character. The narrative form demands that the narrator present a sympathetic hero who moves the plot along. A narrator must create and present a self in the story's events (in the past) that bears a credible relationship to him/herself in the storytelling event (in the present). Audience members similarly must reconcile the narrator and protagonist. In professional development and inquiry groups, part-time speech communities that consciously attend to the importance of conversation and story, it can be inferred that narrators pay special attention to the creation and presentation of narrated selves. Here I explore this issue of presentation of self through two oral personal experience stories I collected in the Lincoln, Nebraska, Teacher Study Group. I speculate on how the context of this professional development and inquiry group allowed the narrators to portray hostile school worlds in their stories and, by implication, their own heroism by enduring everyday hostility. I lastly address how this then presents a problem to groups nominally about teacher development.

PERSONAL NARRATIVE FORM AND PRESENTATION OF SELVES

I begin with the assumption that the personal experience narrative is an expressive form. We may be inclined to see, and respect, teachers' reflections on their experiences as story. We do tend as sympathetic listeners to hear stories when people talk about their teaching lives. It is related to what Bruner (1986) calls the narrative mode of thought that is part of our cultural-psychological makeup. But, textually speaking, reflection upon experience is not necessarily story of experience.

Genre Concerns

Folklorist Sandra Stahl (1989), who has studied most thoroughly everyday personal narratives as oral literature, concludes that the personal experience narrative has three features that together define it as a genre and make it distinct from other forms of narrative. First, like all narratives, personal experience narratives need some dramatic narrative structure. They must have something resembling a beginning, middle, and end; complicating action; and some sort of resolution. Second, personal experience narratives are implicitly "true"; they are understood to be expressly nonfictional. Third, the personal experience narrator is also the main character in the story she or he is telling. Structurally speaking, the narrator is the "hero" of her or his own story, what Stahl calls the "self-same" of the narrator and protagonist.

The genre of the personal narrative hangs on this third attribute. Other narrative forms can be about purportedly true events, but they do not require narrator involvement as dramatis persona (e.g., legends, family stories). Or they can involve the narrator and not be expressly true (e.g., jokes). In the personal experience narrative, the narrator offers her or his involvement in the story's events as "the primary means of certifying the truth of the incident upon which the story is based" (Stahl, 1989, pp. 18–19). Moreover, as a character in her or his own story, the narrator vouches that the events were not only real, but also dramatic and story-worthy.

Oral Narration Concerns

The personal experience narrator's task is further complicated by the situated, oral nature of the narration in contexts like professional development and inquiry groups. Erving Goffman (1959) first articulated how we are continually in a process of presenting a self in social settings, managing the impressions we offer to others as a way to fashion an identity. Telling stories is one way in which we present ourselves to others (Young, 1987). Oral personal experience narratives entail tellings with an immediate audience, even if it is one person. The narrator operates in the here and now of the narrative event *and* in the purported past of the story's event. The narrator is thus in a process of simultaneously presenting him/herself as storyteller *in the narrative present* and as story character *in the narrated past*. Another way of putting this is that a personal experience narrator is presenting a *narrative self* and a *narrated self*.

This presents a double-sided, interactive task in social settings like professional development and inquiry groups. The narrator must make a credible connection between the *narrative* and *narrated* selves. The narrator must present these selves as integratable to audience members. The audience similarly is presented with the task of integrating the two selves presented in storytelling, actively searching for the congruence between the selves. As Stahl (1989) says, "[B]ecause I know that the teller *is or was* the character . . . my response [to the story] must integrate at least these two images of the teller, [and] the integration necessarily creates a dynamic character in my mind" (pp. 22, emphasis in original). The narrator and audience are undoubtedly aware of this interplay. Moreover, since this involves telling "true" stories, it entails managing an impression of truthfulness. In everyday parlance, it is called the need to be honest.

Local Limits on Heroism

All narrative involves some degree of exaggeration or falsification (Stahl, 1989). Stories are not the events or experiences they recount, but representations of those events and experiences through narrative form. Oral narratives of personal experience are exaggerated dramas. A narrator is thus limited by the perception of the acceptable limits of exaggeration of the narrated self. These limits are shared and produced by the ongoing negotiation within a group of interlocutors. Contexts determine how much a narrator can exaggerate the dramatic rendering of events and consequently the attenuation of her or his role as hero, effectively putting limits on the kinds of heroes one can present in one's stories. Some settings allow for, even encourage, great exaggeration of the events and the narrator's role in those events (e.g., adolescent friendship groups). Other settings may allow for "just the facts" and inhibit excessive exaggeration of the events (e.g., elementary classrooms that emphasize the literality of student experience in oral and written narration, in which students are instructed to "tell the truth"). The narrator must be mindful of local limits, avoiding making her/himself appear an overly extravagant hero. But she or he also must be concerned with telling a good story, with sufficient drama, and take care to not present a flabby and unsympathetic hero. These demands tug at each other and require the narrator to strategically attend to these limits of the narrated self.

In contexts like professional development and inquiry groups, the participants come to know each other well. In the Lincoln Teacher Study Group, for instance, members have knowledge of each other's school lives through long-standing friendships, professional affiliations, collegial contact within schools and districts, or university coursework. More broadly, they share social histories and frames of reference in their institutional roles as public school educators, which lends a sense of "knowing what it is like" to be a teacher. A personal experience narrator in a professional development and inquiry group must not only integrate features of truthfulness and drama in her or his stories, as demanded by the genre, but must work to maintain a convincing credibility as an educator who is a member of the group, known to others, *and* the hero in the story she or he is telling.

THE TEACHER STUDY GROUP AS A STORYTELLING CONTEXT

As of the spring of 1999, we were still an elementary teacher group composed of five regular members, all from the Lincoln, Nebraska, area. Since the fall of 1996, we had met monthly during the academic year, in members' homes, usually over dinner. I knew two of the members, Vera and Seth, from having worked with them and their students on community inquiry. They knew the other members I mention below. I asked these teachers to come together for friendly conversation about their work with children, what they saw as obstacles to doing the work they wanted to do and the teachers they wanted to become, and so that we might be able to create a nonschool site to learn about teaching from other practitioners.

Group Membership

Vera and Seth are both fifth-grade teachers at the same elementary school, which is considered "urban," with substantial numbers of low-income and minority children. Sam is a second-year teacher at a large elementary school in a working-class residential area. He was a teacher education student in Vera's classroom 2 years earlier. Molly is a third-grade teacher, with 13 years experience, at a very large school with a substantial upper-middle-class population, which she describes as "competition happy" with parents "always wanting to know how their kid stands in [academic] relation to other kids." Dana teaches in a second/third-grade split classroom and has 7 years experience at a school similar to Molly's. Seth and Dana have known each other since they were in a teacher education program together. I am the only member not currently an elementary teacher, although I was one prior to becoming a teacher educator. We have occasional members, but these five and myself form the core.

Teaching Against the Grain and Marginality

Many of my Sustainable Teacher Learning and Research network colleagues formed groups around such substantive dimensions as subject matter and gender concerns. However, I formed the Teacher Study Group with no other agenda than bringing together teachers who seemed to be thoughtful or, in David Cohen's (1988) word, "adventurous." My experience indicated to me that such teachers describe their work or their pedagogical goals as "child-centered" and "risk taking," as resisting conventional practice, or "teaching against the grain," as Marilyn Cochran-Smith (1991) puts it. It was my assumption that such teachers consciously and conscientiously struggle with the constraints of a nineteenth-century institutional structure with centralized and top-down administration and policies that confound their relationships with children in the world of ideas. I further assumed, along with my forbears and contemporaries in progressive education, that such teachers have managed to agitate or disrupt some aspect of school culture, for which they may have paid a personal and professional price. This often entails some form of marginalization as a result of questioning their school's policies and practices. For instance, Vera tells how she continues to annoy her principal and colleagues by stating frankly that standardized reading tests do not reliably reflect her or anyone else's students' reading abilities. Moreover, she indicates how such tests can portray low-income and minority students as inferior. In so doing she calls attention to the potentially racist implications in a "test-obsessed" school district, and consequently is treated "as some kind of nut."

This is not to say that these teachers either see or present themselves as "radicals" who are careless in their criticism of school policies and practices. To do so, they *all* state, might put their jobs at risk. And they all lament their own acquiescence to the "system." However, they express a kind of consciousness about the organization of schooling as contributing to difficulties in teaching practice. Individually and collectively in meetings, they note that educational problems do not reside solely within individual children. They share some notion, reflected in their stories and conversations in Teacher Study Group meetings, of the slippery but real institutional obstacles to becoming child-centered. For instance, centralized curriculum and its enforcement through grade-level teams and testing mitigate against their abilities to, as Seth puts it, "respond to the kids' interests, and who they really are, not what the standardized curriculum thinks they are." Members occasionally may raise this in the contexts of their schools, with colleagues and administrators, but they say they get the message that they are undermining their schools, "not being team players" in Dana's words. It is this sense of pervasive collegial and administrative pressure to conform that infuses the majority of Teacher Study Group stories.

Marginality and Teacher Development

For me, the teachers' sense of marginality made for an interesting professional development opportunity in a professional development and inquiry group: to be in sympathetic company with like-minded educators. Together with the above assumptions, I felt these teachers could form their own agendas for the group's meetings and define what they wanted from their gathering. Moreover, their gathering offered an opportunity to hear great teacher stories. Folklorists have long told us that individuals who experience marginality, and collectively perceive some threat to their existence, often will come together and develop expressive practices, such as storytelling, as ways to make sense out of the world, learn from others, and find psychic security in solidarity (see Toelken, 1996).

The agendas of the Teacher Study Group have been inconsistent or nonexistent. We have read and discussed Herbert Kohl's book *The Discipline of Hope* (1998). We have tried to make an effort to come to meetings with a story about a particular child, with a half-hearted goal of making this a "child study" group. But the group has emerged as a place to vent and release frustration with sympathetic company. That is, the talk involves mostly the telling of stories that are targeted at colleagues and administrators who do not think or teach like the storytellers do. I take it as a measure of their own anger in their school lives that they use the group this way; through conversation and story they objectify their school world and criticize it as repressive to their being. Thus the focus or theme of the group has become "release." Whether catharsis is relevant to professional development poses a problem that I take up at the end of the chapter.

GROUP ETHOS AND DISCURSIVE RULES

Flowing from the shared value of "child-centeredness," the Teacher Study Group has become a sphere in which the participants' talk—their conversations and stories—is predominantly around their adult relationships at their schools, most significantly with colleagues and administrators. Less frequently, and only recently, have these teachers begun to discuss their relationships with their students. In general, this group is composed of individuals who identify themselves and each other as "progressive" or "child-centered teachers." They present themselves, in group meetings and in one-on-one interviews and conversations with me, as educators who want "to see children as the center of their curricula" and, in what has become a common refrain, whose "work begins with kids."

Discursively Enacted Values

This is not to say that their actual work and practices perfectly enact these values. My study of the talk in our group is not directed toward checking to see whether their conversations and stories correspond to their work, whether they are somehow living up to the values and goals of child-centeredness. This might force me into some deficit modeling (i.e., discovering they are not really the progressive pedagogues they claim to be) or some ugly detective work, checking on the truthfulness of their stories. Child-centeredness itself is not an unproblematic notion, lending itself to versions and permutations that may deconstruct. My concern, rather, is with how these expressed values operate as discursive aspects of this group's life, in which members present and narrate themselves as teachers who, if they do not enact the values of child-centeredness, state openly that they believe in them and that they see them as dispositions to aspire to.

Consequently, the talk in this group has come to involve conversation and story about what members describe as obstacles and impediments to their enacting this belief in/aspiration to child-centeredness. Specifically, this involves their relationships with other adults in their schools who act, directly or indirectly, as obstacles and impediments. It also involves almost exclusively critical talk about school colleagues, team members, principals, and assistant principals. While parents and office staff are mentioned in my data, the overwhelming foci are struggles with colleagues who are impediments to group members becoming the teachers they want to become and obstacles to the child-centered teaching they claim they want to do. The conversation thus sounds very critical, often harsh, and sometimes cruel. For instance, the use of rather unkind nick-names that reflect physical and personality traits has become common. Seth's story involving an agitated janitor, "a postal worker waiting to happen," reflects this.

Rules of and for Conversation and Story

This overarching ethos that identifies this group can be translated into an emergent series of interrelated rules of and for talk in the group, above and beyond the general rules for conversation (turn taking) and story (the genre features of personal experience narrative). These are implicit or local cultural rules, rather than explicit or contracted ones. One over-arching rule involves not criticizing children or students directly. That is, it is unacceptable for a member of the Teacher Study Group to express in meetings overt criticism toward her or his own, or anyone's else's, students, like that which is expressed about colleagues and administra-tors. When this rule is disregarded, and a member complains about a struggle with a particular child, this is always accompanied by an apology, for example, "I'm sorry, I know I should not think that way," which indicates awareness of the rule to not be "anti-kid."

Conversely, a speaker in the Teacher Study Group must make an effort to express "concern" for children. Even the extremely troublesome students must be talked about in sympathetic or empathic ways, for example, "Can you imagine what it must be like for that kid?" Sam told a story of his losing control of a situation in disciplining a boy in his classroom. After blaming himself (not the kid, who swore at him) for the problem, which landed him in his principal's office for a quiet dressing down, he went on to say that he wondered what it must be like at home for a kid like that to confront him as a male authority figure, and wondered whether he was not merely the target of "displaced anger." While it is possible to laud Sam as an individual for being reflective and thoughtful, which he undoubtedly seems to be, this also indicates the power of the rules in this discursive context. I could imagine another setting where "kid-bashing" would be perfectly acceptable for children who were "disci-pline problems."

Similarly, this concern for children is extended to parents when they are the objects of conversation and story. Parents are to be criticized only when they act as obstacles similar to colleagues (e.g., the nosy parent who continually questions and speaks down to the teacher). When parents are criticized, this criticism also is accompanied by an apology. Molly, for instance, tells stories of a wealthy mother of one of her students who does not work, and finds much time to visit in the classroom under the guise of watching her son. This mother eventually, in Molly's stories, will report to other mothers and make "suggestions" not only to Molly but to her principal about how she ought to change her practices. Molly works to contain her frustration and says, "They are mothers and have the right to be concerned about their kids. But it does make my life hard being under suspicion."

There are also rules about how to treat the utterances of others in the group. A member must not criticize others in the group. That is, one must not directly challenge others' assertions about their work, the veracity of their stories, or the overall interpretation of school events, personnel, or activities. Occasionally a challenge emerges, almost always around how a child is depicted in a story. When this happens, there is invariably a relatively long and uncomfortable silence, where another turn at talk normally would occur, before the conversation resumes. Some discursive mechanisms have emerged to contain the conflict, such as telling the speaker who has been challenged that she or he is undoubtedly correct in her or his interpretation. As one member said immediately after a challenge, "I was just looking at it another way." Whenever this happens, there are rarely any further challenges during the remainder of the meeting.

This relates to another rule—that members must express "support" for other members as they discuss and tell stories of their struggles. This involves direct utterances of sympathy and empathy (e.g., "I am so sorry," and "I've had that feeling before"), as well as more subtle or indirect responses, such as affirmative nodding of the head and, "Oh no," and "Oh my God," affable "backchanneling" in sociolinguistic terms.

Like all local sociolinguistic rules, these are not always explicit and involve a tacit understanding and agreement. Such implicit understanding of local cultural rules of and for discursive participation does not reduce the interlocutors to unthinking automatons. Local cultural rule following is not an obvious activity, but a tacit one. Cultural rules are not rules if they dogmatically determine how we use them. Members of the Teacher Study Group must have *a sense of* the rules in order to participate competently as discursive members of the group.

As these rules apply to storytelling, they allow a backdrop and a sympathetic environment for the telling of stories of members' experiences, where they are supported and empathized with. By keeping criticisms of children and parents off limits, what remain are stories about teachers, administrators, and school staff who impede the teacher members in what they say they want to become. It is to instances of these stories that I now turn.

TWO TEACHER STUDY GROUP STORIES

The following stories were gathered in the same meeting in late September 1997. It was our second meeting of the year and we were into the fifth or sixth week of the local school calendar. The tone of the meeting was characteristically cathartic, with a releasing of pent-up frustration. The fall in Nebraska can still be intolerably hot and humid. It was as if the heat and humidity had already ratcheted up the frustration for Teacher Study Group members early in the school year.

THIS IS NOT YOUR SCHOOL

By Seth

SETH: Yeah, I didn't tell you about it. That mother fucking custodian Fred today.

VERA: Oh, yeah, you know that Fred freaked out in your room?

SETH: I know.

VERA: He put all your kids on "step ten" and I left. And I was like—he started slamming windows and I went, "Ooh, he's goin', he's blown a gasket." And Roger and William [Seth's students] were in there and they were being really good. And I went, "Wheeoo!"

SETH: They were being good? Because, I mean, I didn't know what the hell's going on.

VERA: Yeah.

DANA: What happened? What's this step stuff?

SETH: I don't know what the fuck this step thing is.

VERA: He made it up in his own head. He has steps for us from last year during the science thing [last year] Seth was on.

DANA: What? When you're on step ten, do you get killed or what?

VERA: He was slamming windows. I was . . .

SETH: He's a postal worker waiting to happen.

VERA: He is. [laughter]

DANA: He came down on your kids for being messy?

SETH: No. I was down on door duty and some of my kids use the phone after school because my room is open, you know. They need to use the phone to call their parents to find out what's going on, get a ride home, or whatever. And I come in the office after school and William and those guys are, "Ah, that phone up there in your room is messed up." And I said, "Why is it messed up?" He goes, "Oh that custodian, he, boy he's mean, he's angry." And Billy and Rich [other custodians] respond, "I wonder why!" to them, you know, obviously saying "Cause it's how you treat him." And so I go upstairs to get my bag and stuff and Fred's in my room, and he walks out kind of all mad and Irv [another custodian] goes, "Jeeze you're slacking, you should be done with your fourth room by now," kind of joking around. And Fred's like, "Not with these . . . " You know, he called them basically degenerates, you know, no good, low-down kids. It was basically . . . and he even said something like, "low-down rude kids."

VERA: They were being absolutely fine. I walked in there looking for you.

SETH: He said they were on the phone using profanity and—and all this. This is what he told Irv. He's walking out and blows past me like I'm just nothing. You know and just blows past me. And Irv's talking to him. And then Damian, Roger, and William start walking towards us. And I go, "Fred, are these the young men you are talking about?" And he goes, "Yeah but you don't say anything because nothing gets done about it and it just doesn't. And it doesn't do any good."

DANA: Oh my God!

SETH: And then I go, "Guys, ah, you gotta start using the office phone. You need to go downstairs. When school's out you're going to start having to leave right away. *This is not your school!* [laughter]. *This is run by custodians*." And then Damian goes, "You need to get my mom a new job." And, ah, cause he's having a hard time getting home with his mom and he's walking away and Irv goes—and this is fucking disgusting—he goes, "What's his mom do?" And of course I respond, you know, it's like these guys are my buddies. Like I give a fuck what these guys say. They're such assholes to kids, you know.

VERA: Oh yeah.

SETH: And then I go, "His mom's a university professor." He goes, "And she's got a hoodlum like that for a son."

DANA: Oh my God.

VERA: Irv said that?

MOLLY: Wow.

SETH: Irv said that. A hoodlum. I wonder why he called him a
hoodlum? Because he's Black? Hmmmmmm, you think so?
[sarcastically]

SETH: Do you think [your son] would be called a hoodlum?

STEVE: He's lucky that way.

VERA: Oh my God.

DANA: Wow. You should document that. You really should document that.

STEVE: That was racist.

SETH: That was racist as shit.

VERA: Oh God, I hate that place.

I HAVE THREE PASSIVE-AGGRESSIVE TEACHERS ON MY TEAM!

By Molly

STEVE: What happened with your team member?

MOLLY: Oh I went in there [her principal's office] with a situation
with one of my team members and she said, "Molly, she realizes she's an E-N-F-C or E-N-F" [acronyms of personality
types derived from a personality inventory used in her school
district].

STEVE: What's the situation? Tell us the situation.

MOLLY: Oh Jasmine, . . . she has been there, the situation was she's
been in the last 3 years. Actually she was there 4 years ago
and then she left to go to City [a school in the district] and
she didn't like City and so she came back. And so anyway,
when I was gone for these 2 weeks [for special team leadership training] I kind of asked her to be in charge, to field questions from team members if there is problems with kids, or
whatever. Well, she took charge all right.

DANA: Are you team leader?

MOLLY: Ah huh. And she decided . . .

VERA: She wouldn't give up her throne or what? [laughter]

MOLLY: She didn't like the way I was doing things and so she got
the team to do things a different way.

STEVE: Her way.

MOLLY: See things her way. And so, when I got back and she was
like, "Well, Molly, we decided not to do this. And we decided
not to do that. Is that okay?" And I am like, "Well, I, you
know, I don't think so. I don't think so." And so anyway with
that situation I went to Carla [her principal]. And she said
"Well, Molly, you realize you're dealing with an E-N-F," you

know whatever, "and so and so is I-N-S-C" [laughter] and all
this stuff.

STEVE: Thanks for the feedback.

SETH: Hey that's enlightening.

MOLLY: I am like yeah, "Fine yeah. Why are you talking with all
these . . . ?" [laughter]

SETH: Freaking acronyms?

DANA: Why speak in acronyms?

MOLLY: So anyway the whole discussion was and it came out
that—that Jasmine is passive-aggressive. I have three passive-
aggressive teachers on my team!

MULTIPLE: [laughter]

MOLLY: I'm like, "I can't do this."

DANA: Out of four?

SETH: Psychologists must make a mint out of schools.

MOLLY: Out of five of us.

DANA: School has very passive-aggressive behavior.

SETH: Oh yeah.

VERA: Oh yeah they do because you know . . .

DANA: Because you're powerless and they get . . .

VERA: Well, angry. You're not supposed to be angry.

MAKING SENSE OF SETH'S AND MOLLY'S STORIES

Molly's and Seth's stories are characteristic of the stories that get told in
the group. Profanity is not uncommon, nor is unqualified anger. Both
these stories are consonant with the general discursive rules in the group.
While there are no children in Molly's story, those in Seth's are portrayed
sympathetically. The adults, janitors, team leaders, and an administrator
are all depicted negatively. In the course of their tellings, neither narrator
is challenged or criticized, and each is overtly supported by utterances
of other members.

More specifically, both of these stories exemplify a common feature
of the Teacher Study Group stories. They involve the depiction, or what
Young (1987) calls the narrative "reconstitution," of school worlds. These
worlds are hostile, to children in Seth's, and especially to teachers in both.

Molly's story involves betrayal by a team colleague, the passive-
aggression of her team members, and the indifference of her administrator.
Each of these are forms of hostility. Molly's sense of hurt from the betrayal
was palpable as she told this story that night. In her story Molly shows
her principal (Carla) as trying to rationalize the betrayal as a result of

personality traits (Molly's reference to acronyms from a personality inventory), not an organizational or institutional problem. The principal cynically frames the team problems as individual psychological problems (which, if logic follows, require therapy, not school leadership). This then makes it Molly's problem to learn to get along, especially since she has been presented with personality inventory data. The hostility of betrayal is extended into the hostility of passive-aggression via Carla's indifference to Molly's plight. Indifference is itself a form of hostility (as Elie Weisel has said repeatedly, the opposite of love is not hate but indifference). All of this adds up to a quietly and indecently hostile place for Molly to teach.

The hostility in Seth's story is much more overt. The narrative is populated by custodians, and one in particular, who are antagonistic to students. The hostility of the janitors, or at least Irv, is racist (I [Steve] assumed Seth knew this when he said it; I responded to make sure that this point came out) and incenses Seth. But Seth not only criticizes janitors. His critique is of how schools are hostile to children of color in multiple ways and, by implication, hostile to teachers, like himself, who take a child-centered perspective. His story is thus about the hostility of the schools as a community ("This is not your school! This is run by custodians"). Moreover, although it is not present in the text, Seth is implicitly criticizing his (and Vera's) school administration. Every member of the Teacher Study Group has told at least one tale of her or his administrators; the context encourages such stories. While his school's administration does not make an appearance in the text of his narrative, when Seth speaks to the hostility of the custodians, who run the school, this is heard in the Teacher Study Group as reflecting permission of the school's administration for this hostility to occur.

Enduring Heroes in Teacher Study Group Stories

What makes these stories relevant to my concern for the presentation of narrative and narrated selves is the pervasive sense of assault that comes through in Seth's and Molly's stories. In their stories, Seth and Molly present themselves as objects or targets of institutional hostility. Their narrated heroism results from their ability to *endure* the hostility. They never really triumph; antagonists are not vanquished. Seth protects his students from the custodians, and Molly is looking to save herself from passive-aggression and indifference. They are virtuous people who "deal with it," and their heroic virtue arises from this ability to weather hostility. Their heroism is thus subtle martyrdom, like someone who takes a punch in the mouth.

The context of the Teacher Study Group encourages and limits this particular kind of heroism in a narrated self. The narrative form *and* the context of the Teacher Study Group encourage the creation of these hostile worlds that a narrator can inhabit as the chief character. Seth and Molly both re-create their school worlds. The Teacher Study Group offers a setting in which they bring forward what otherwise may go unsaid among friends and colleagues. These stories offer them the opportunity to demonstrate their resolve or personal constitution to withstand the hostility and assaults on their aspirations. They do not come right out and say, "Janitors and team members prevent me from teaching in particular ways." Rather, they convey the indirect, almost existential sense in which their senses of self and values are under attack in their institutions. Telling stories is a way to be heroic in school worlds that won't let them be heroes. These heroes have credibility in the group. Though exaggerated dramas, they fit with the ethos of the group. Seth and Molly manage the impression of truthfulness in great part due to the supportive nature of the group. They are not challenged and they know, generally speaking, they will not be challenged, and thus have the comfort of literary license. Their narrated and narrative selves cohere.

Story as a "Talking Cure"

There is almost a psychotherapeutic character to this kind of discourse and storytelling in this professional development and inquiry group. Being with sympathetic others, who encourage the naming of hostile school worlds in and through story, offers Teacher Study Group members a way of making sense of their own personal school experience. If Teacher Study Group members' own sense of vocational identity is bound up in what they take to be "child-centeredness," if their institutions are directly or indirectly hostile to this goal, and if their own sense of alienation derives from this hostility, then a professional development and inquiry group can serve an important function for some teachers. It seems important to attend to the sense of alienation or marginalization that members feel, a kind of psychological "need" that must be addressed before we ask teachers to consider development. It thus would seem that an opportunity to connect with others, and to deal with anger and cynicism, is important if we are to move on to a state where teachers are ready to act affirmatively.

DILEMMA FOR A PROFESSIONAL DEVELOPMENT AND INQUIRY GROUP

While I think there are clearly some psychic benefits for the members of the Teacher Study Group in meeting, having conversations, and telling stories like Molly's and Seth's, I am left with some nagging concerns about the faith that we put into story as a practice for professional development in conversation-based groups, and specifically what the Teacher Study Group has become. To proceed with the therapeutic analogy, I am reminded of when I was a social worker dealing with families, and my first supervisor asserted persuasively that "insight therapy does not work!" He was making the point that learning that you have a problem harbors no plan of action for dealing with the problem. In fact, it may make things worse, leading to a greater sense of helplessness and an incapacity to make a change.

Confronting Naive Faith in Story

Similarly, I am left asking myself questions about the Teacher Study Group: What kind of story is being told here? What kind of heroes are we asking people to be in their stories? We assume, as teacher developers, that storytelling is a form of sense making or inquiry into experience. And we encourage teachers to tell stories of personal experience in group settings. Can the narrative form by itself be transformative? Is simply telling stories sufficient to encourage or induce members to work toward making changes, to work toward their stated values, aspirations, and goals as educators?

My concerns arise from the common stories that are being told in the Teacher Study Group, of which Seth's and Molly's are representative. By credibly narrating a hostile world and one's endurance in it, are we not taking for granted that world? Does not the narrative need that kind of world if we are to have heroes who *endure*? In other words, by telling these stories of unchanging hostile school worlds, are we not reifying those worlds? If so, we effectively are limiting ourselves in imagining what might be possible. Dare I suggest that the telling of personal experience narratives may confine or restrict how we might think about improving our lot in schools?

Narratively Maintaining Hostile School Worlds

What I am suggesting is that the very thing that gives the Lincoln Teacher Study Group strength may be its chief drawback. The group meetings offer a temporary but important refuge to the core members. They can sit, have a meal, and enjoy the company of those with whom they share something in common not only in occupation but in outlook. They find comfort in telling and hearing stories of their hostile school worlds, and they communicate to one another, "You are not alone. I too feel under assault in my school." Yet in order to accomplish this, they need to tell a story in a particular way. In doing so they may be reifying, through their stories and their credible heroic roles in them, the existing school structure. What would the hero look like if she or he could get her or his way and remove the obstacles and become fully "child-centered"? I am not saying that they want their schools to stay the way they are. After all, these school worlds are hostile. Rather, by telling this kind of story, they may contribute to keeping schools the way they are. We unwittingly may be assisting the limiting, not liberating, effect of narrative. The general story that they are sharing is one of living in a system incapable of change; all that one can do is endure it.

I am not the first to point out the limiting effect of narrative (see Florio-Ruane, 1997). However, I think it important to consider the limiting effect in the very concrete circumstances of professional development and inquiry groups, groups that are dedicated to teacher development, not teacher inertia. This is both an empirical question—What are the stories being told in these groups?—and a development question—Are the stories of self and experience in any sense transformative?

POSTSCRIPT: TELLING NEW STORIES

I am confessing to my own collusion in the current state of the Teacher Study Group. I had been taking a hands-off approach, following my commitment to letting teachers take the lead in the group. However, groups take on a life of their own, above and beyond what any one individual may want in and from a group.

In the spring of 1999, I raised my concern with the state of the Teacher Study Group with Seth. Seth had emerged as the leader of the group, organizing meeting times, keeping in touch with members, and leading conversations. Seth agreed with me that we had been telling the same story and that lately the group seemed to be a place for unproductive complaint. He put it like this:

> It is good that we can come together and bitch about our schools because they can be dehumanizing places. But it is strange that we never get around to talking about kids, even though we say we are into kids. It is getting tiring and I am not sure that it is making much of a difference in our work to leave it at bitching.

We agreed that we ought to try having an agenda for each meeting, laid out well in advance. We would still encourage stories, but we would conscientiously encourage stories around the agenda topics. I suggested that the new Nebraska state standards could offer such a focus for the entire school year. Seth responded enthusiastically.

In our last meeting in May 1999, I proposed that during the 1999–2000 academic year we use our monthly meetings to discuss specifically the new Nebraska state standards, and that we think about how to cope with them as teachers because they cannot be ignored. I indicated that I was certain their schools and districts would begin to implement these standards and inform their teachers how to think about and use them. I felt it was the professional thing to do, to be informed and prepared to critique the standards, how they might affect any move toward child-centeredness, and how teachers might respond thoughtfully. My proposal was accepted enthusiastically. I told the group that we could use this opportunity to "tell a new story," one that might serve more activist ends, rather than reifying the existing structure through our stories.

We have yet to meet in the 1999–2000 year due to a turn of events that involves a key member of the Teacher Study Group. Seth has taken a leave from his school to teach language arts methods in a regional teacher education program. In the fall, with two other teachers, he sent out an announcement, asking for local progressive teachers to meet in a colloquy to "talk, remember, and share visions of our futures." In this e-mail communiqué he alluded to the Teacher Study Group, saying that "by us just meeting as teachers we are doing something." Yet his message called for something larger and more action-oriented. His words speak for themselves:

> Many teachers recently have come to face a sense of isolation, humility about their teaching practices and a loss of voice in curricular decisions. These teachers are losing their voice in bettering their practices and responding to children's learning. I have colleagues that are feeling overwhelmed in an environment of school reform that rejects teacher knowledge and passions for public schooling.

His words combine some of the virtues of the Teacher Study Group (addressing alienation), the implied dissatisfaction we have had with the state of the group, and a desire for some action. He goes on to say that "excellent teachers are feeling terrible about their practices" and are "disjointed." He concludes by asking: "What if we inquired into the knowledge of local teachers?" and "Could we as a collective group bridge an understanding for ourselves, young teachers, retired teachers and communities of what our schools could possibly be?"

This message is suffused with hope and lacks the complaint he and I cited the previous spring. We discussed using our Teacher Study Group's upcoming conversations of the new state standards as one site of several to achieve the goal of his call to action, possibly with some new members. Here seems to be an opportunity to tell a new story, to draw from the Teacher Study Group's quasi-psychotherapeutic salve, and to act upon child-centered aspirations. I have no idea what will happen, but we may have a new kind of hero in our own stories.

REFERENCES

Bruner, J. (1986). *Actual minds, possible worlds*. Cambridge, MA: Harvard University Press.

Cochran-Smith, M. (1991). Learning to teach against the grain. *Harvard Educational Review, 61*(2), 279–310.

Cohen, D. K. (1988). Teaching practice: Plus ça change . . . In P. W. Jackson (Ed.), *Contributing to educational change: Perspectives on research and practice* (pp. 27–84). Berkeley: McCutcheon.

Florio-Ruane, S. (1997). To tell a new story: Reinventing narratives of culture, identity, and education. *Anthropology and Education Quarterly, 28*(2), 152–162.

Goffman, E. (1959). *The presentation of self in everyday life*. New York: Anchor Books.

Kohl, H. (1998). *The discipline of hope: Learning from a lifetime of teaching*. New York: Simon & Schuster.

Stahl, S. D. (1989). *Literary folkloristics and the personal narrative*. Bloomington: Indiana University Press.

Toelken, B. (1996). *The dynamics of folklore*. Logan: Utah State University Press.

Young, K. (1987). *Taleworlds and storyrealms: The phenomenology of narrative*. Dordrecht, Netherlands: Martins Nijhoff.

CHAPTER 7

Connected Conversations:
Forms and Functions of Teacher Talk

Lynne Cavazos & The Members of WEST

THIS CHAPTER IS REALLY a set of related stories, stitched together like squares of a quilt. The stories show and tell us about the different forms and functions of teacher talk enacted among women science teachers in Santa Barbara, California, during the group's first 3 years of operation. Beyond distinguishing forms and functions of teacher talk, the chapter also identifies three dilemmas faced by the Women Educators of Science and Technology (WEST) that will likely challenge other teacher conversation groups as well.

MAKING CONNECTIONS BY SHARING OUR LIVES

Stories are about interconnections—connections between my life and someone else's; between the past and present; between the stories of our lives and the stories of our teaching; between the larger narratives which make up life. These connections make up stories our lives tell.
—C. Chambers, "Looking for a Home"

Storytelling is part of the daily lives of teachers. It is the most common way teachers communicate with one another about their evolving, personal, and practical knowledge. Teachers' stories are part of the living conversation of a school community, and sharing them is a natural way for teachers to enter into one another's lives. When a teacher shares a story, it is a "password" into an inclusive community of school folklorists and known only to those who share the same social horizon (Casey, 1993). The folklore of teachers, referred to by Schubert and Ayers (1992) as "teacher lore," weaves together the life experiences of teachers and highlights the knowledge and ways of knowing they share and understand.

The organization of space, time, and tasks for teachers, however, seriously hinders their ability to have meaningful conversations about their teaching (Little, 1990). The stories that teachers share are often told indirectly and informally during moments between classes, over lunch, or during extracurricular activities after school hours. It would be more accurate to call these brief exchanges of information "snippets—little clipped versions of teaching and learning" (Schubert & Ayers, 1992, p. 12)—rather than stories, since they are often incomplete, fragmented, and lacking the traditional elements of a story: time, place, plot, and scene (Connelly & Clandinin, 1990). Rarely does a teacher have the time to retell and expand one of these clipped versions of personal experience. Consequently, the significance of these snippets of knowledge is left unexplored, their underlying meaning unrevealed.

The school setting often is not a safe place to share one's personal and professional life. Most schools do not provide a private, risk-free setting for two or more women teachers to share their knowledge, raise questions, and examine current pedagogical strategies. The risk occurs because talk often is misconstrued or misinterpreted when overheard by others. The faculty lounge, staff lunchroom, and even teachers' classrooms are not risk-free settings and certainly could not be classified as private space. Space for teachers often resembles a busy hotel lobby: a continuous stream of people in and out asking questions, making phone calls, looking for lost items, catching up on the latest bits of news from the morning newscast or local paper. For a woman teacher to become a reflective practitioner the setting has to feel safe, and she must trust that her colleagues will be supportive and nonjudgmental if useful conversations are to take place.

Empowering Women Science Teachers to Tell Their Stories

Empowering relationships develop over time and it takes time for participants to recognize the value that the relationship holds. Empowering rela-

tionships involve feelings of "connectedness" that are developed in a situation of equality, caring and mutual purpose and intention.
—P. Hogan, *A Community of Teacher Researchers*

What kind of setting fosters care, concern, and connection, and provides women with the opportunity to experience an empowering relationship with other teachers? The answer to this question came from several research studies conducted by feminist researchers using methodologies that were voice-centered and relational in approach and firmly grounded in girls' and women's lives and ways of knowing.

In a Different Voice (Gilligan, 1982), *Making Connections* (Gilligan, Lyons, & Hanmer, 1990), *Women's Ways of Knowing* (Belenky, Clinchy, Goldberger, & Tarule, 1986), and *Meeting at the Crossroads* (Brown & Gilligan, 1992) are four influential research studies that identify strategies that empower girls and women to talk with courage. Their approaches entail "listening to girls and women as authorities about their own experiences and representing their voices in a written text" (Rogers, 1993, p. 267). The relationship is empowering for the participants because they are given the freedom to speak their minds and to have their words, their interpretations, taken seriously.

Based on the work of these women researchers, WEST was formed in 1996 to provide a feminist approach to professional development that would emphasize teacher talk and teacher-to-teacher dialogue within a community setting. With the exception of Melissa, the women in WEST are graduates of the Single Subject Teacher Credential Program at the University of California, Santa Barbara, with Lynne as their science methods and procedures instructor and supervisor. Melissa was not a credential student, but rather worked with Lynne as a science supervisor in 1993–94.

The invitation to participate in WEST was offered to women who graduated from UCSB in secondary science education since 1993; only two women declined the invitation to join the group. The two who decided not to participate faced a long commute to the meetings and issues of child care. The original group consisted of 10 women teaching secondary science in Santa Barbara and Ventura Counties. We are diverse in our social, cultural, and economic backgrounds and in our life experiences as women, scientists, and teachers.

Table 7.1 summarizes our histories and characteristics and will help readers understand the standpoints from which the women of WEST interpret the experiences of their lives. The term *standpoint* refers not to a theory but rather to a subjective context in which a person interprets and understands life experiences (Novak, 1978).

Table 7.1. WEST Group Participants

Name and Age	Personal Background	Educational Background	Professional Experience
Lynne Cavazos (51)	Born and raised in rural Michigan; middle-class farming family; divorced with no children, 3 cats; loves to golf, run, and ocean kayak	B.A. in biology, MSU; master's in science education, U of M; Ph.D. in teacher preparation and staff development, MSU	22 years of high school science teaching experience and 7 years in teacher education; coordinator of SPSI & TEP; BTSA director, Santa Barbara County
Marilyn Garza (33)	Grew up in Seattle, WA; eldest of 3 children; married with one toddler; loves to read, watch movies, and play volleyball	B.S. in materials engineering, master's in education, UCSB	5 years of junior high school teaching experience, cooperating teacher, Science Department chair
Melissa Kehl (34)	Born and raised on Staten Island, New York; youngest of 4 children; married with twin babies; enjoys wine tasting and eating sushi	B.S. in biology, Purdue; master's in science education, UCSB	9 years of junior and high school teaching experience, cooperating teacher, 1 year as supervisor for student teachers
Adela Laband (41)	Born and raised in Northern California; from a large middle-class suburban family; married with one teenage stepchild; loves gardening, windsurfing, and car-camping	B.A. in biology, master's in education, UCSB	5 years of junior high school teaching experience, cooperating teacher, MESA advisor
Erin Messersmith (26)	Born in Monarch Beach, CA, but spent part of childhood overseas; avid swimmer and diver, loves playing clarinet	B.S. in biology, master's in education, UCSB	3 years of high school teaching experience
Olga Nikitin (28)	Born and raised in the Ukraine; immigrated with family to the U.S. in 1993; married with no children; loves cooking, needlepoint, and travel	Diploma and M.A. in physics education, Odessa State University; master's in education, UCSB	1 year of high school teaching experience; 3 years experience in creating educational software for ELL students

(Continued)

Table 7.1. *(Continued)*

Name and Age	Personal Background	Educational Background	Professional Experience
Melanie Pearlman (25)	Born on the East Coast and transplanted to California. Recently married; enjoys hiking and playing guitar	B.S. in physics, master's in education, UCSB; summer research apprentice in electrical engineering	3 years of high school teaching experience in physics, cooperating teacher
Mika Shibuya (27)	Born in Saigon; lived in Japan until age 8, immigrated to U.S. in 1980; enjoys swing dancing, playing piano and guitar, and singing	B.S. in biology, master's in education, UCSB; working on CLAD	3 years of middle school teaching; AVID coordinator for school site
April Torres (26)	Born in Missouri, raised in California; Christian family with 1 sister; married with 2 children; enjoys playing the piano, quilting, being a good wife and mother	B.A. in biological science, master's in education, UCSB	2 years of middle school teaching experience in life and physical sciences
Betsy Villalpando (28)	Born and raised in San Diego, CA; 1 of 4 children in a middle-class family; married with no children, 3 cats, and 2 bunnies; loves car-camping, reading, and watching movies	B.A. in physics education, Humbolt State; master's in education, UCSB	4 years of high school teaching experience in physics and integrated science
Andrea "Nea" Voss (30)	Born in Hamburg, Germany; professional family that immigrated to the U.S.; single mother with 3-year-old son; loves to hike and bike	B.S. in environmental biology, California State University, Northridge; master's in education, UCSB	4 years of teaching experience at junior high school and alternative schools
Debby West (32)	Southern California native; middle-class suburban family of 6; single; enjoys scuba diving, backpacking, travel, kayaking; loves strawberries	B.A. in environmental studies, master's in education, UCSB	5 years of junior and high school teaching experience

The motivation of each teacher to join the WEST group varies according to personal and professional needs. Still, in their responses to questions of motivation, all highlight the importance of ongoing support as teachers transition from teacher education programs to the culture of secondary schools:

> I enjoy the support of friends and enjoy talking with women with similar backgrounds. (Betsy)

> WEST provides a safe space for me to talk and express my opinions and ideas. I do not feel heard or respected when I talk with colleagues at school—they make me feel incompetent when I ask questions or make suggestions about curriculum and teaching strategies. (April)

> WEST is an idea factory where I can bounce ideas around and seek solutions for my struggles, discover ways of coping, and learn from colleagues that have similar situations and philosophies of teaching and learning. (Adela)

> It is easy to become isolated in schools and so I enjoy the opportunity to listen to women from other schools and areas of science. The focus on creating innovative curriculum is interesting to me. (Marilyn)

> I feel I can be grounded here. Our shared educational philosophy just feels right to me. (Debby)

> The group provides me with a way to stay connected to science teaching and secondary classrooms. It is exciting to work with women who are exploring ways to reach all students and help them make connections to science. (Lynne)

An Inclusive Community of Women Storytellers

Marni Pearce (1993) provides an image of an ideal inclusive place:

> *INCLUSION*
>
> Inclusion is not "us and them"
> or even "you and me."
>
> It is a smile of recognition, a reassuring touch,
> a sense of genuine belonging.

It is a place where souls can meet
and share and experience
and lives can intermingle.

It is identity.
It is acceptance.
It is a haven for all.

Take my hand;
We can go there together. (p. 2)

The WEST conversation community has become such a place—a place where "women's talk" is accepted and respected; where women's stories and ways of talking are the dominant discourse; where new narratives of women's lives emerge as we exchange stories and talk collectively about our ambitions, possibilities, and accomplishments. We provide support and encouragement for one another and share insights, skills, and strategies for dealing with problematic situations and dilemmas. Together we have created a collective sense of power and authority.

Certainly the composition of a conversation group is critical if it is to be a caring community that encourages participants to engage in serious, thoughtful reflection about their lives as women, as scientists, and as teachers. The decision to invite only women to join the WEST group was purposeful and based on a belief that women can be more courageous, outspoken, and honest in the good company of supportive women science teachers.

Carolyn Heilbrun's (1988) book, *Writing a Woman's Life,* provides support for the decision we made to keep WEST an exclusively female community. According to Heilbrun:

> Female narratives will not find their way into texts if they do not begin in oral exchanges among women in groups hearing and talking to one another. As long as women are isolated one from the other, not allowed to offer other women the most personal accounts of their lives; they will not be part of any narrative of their own. (p. 46)

Although we think it might be possible for female narratives to emerge from gender-mixed storytelling communities, we know that many women will not risk telling a personal experience story for fear of being "put down" by a male colleague or administrator. Some women have the impression, and often justifiably so, that men are unable or unwilling to take them seriously. This is especially true in situations where women are greatly outnumbered by men, as in most science departments. This is not to say that women never share personal stories with men, but when they do, it is because they have developed a relationship of care and equality.

Margaret Yocum (1985) contends that finding women's personal narratives does not depend on physical location or sexual exclusivity. Rather, it depends on

> a mode of social interaction, a space where none need fear ridicule or embarrassment, where participants feel they all share several bonds, where narratives emphasize those bonds, and where each participant is seen as equally capable of and willing to contribute personal information. (p. 52)

THE FUNCTIONS OF TEACHER TALK

The educational knowledge teachers possess about what it means to teach and to learn is embedded within their stories. This knowledge becomes most visible and tangible when teachers have the opportunity to communicate with others in a form of teacher-to-teacher dialogue that encourages reflection, reassessment, and renewed hope for ways to improve professionally and personally.

The women of WEST constructed a visual representation of the practical and theoretical functions of the teacher talk that occurs during our monthly conversations (Figure 7.1). The three concentric circles portray the essential components necessary for our group to learn and develop as a community. The *Three C's of care, concern, and connection* are primary and situated at the center of the model, with *common ground* and a *framework* forming the middle and outer circles. We believe all three circles are essential to create a safe space for optimal conversation and growth.

Inner Circle: Care, Concern, Connection

The three C's of care, concern, and connection represent a trio of qualities first introduced in the work of philosopher Jane Roland Martin (1987). We have adopted her terms and created descriptions meaningful to our specific conversation group. Melissa, an experienced teacher in the group, provides this interpretation:

> At the core of the model are the three C's. All three are crucial for the success of our group. It is like a three-legged chair, if one leg is missing, it will no longer be functional. Care is the first of the three C's because without it, there would be no listening. The

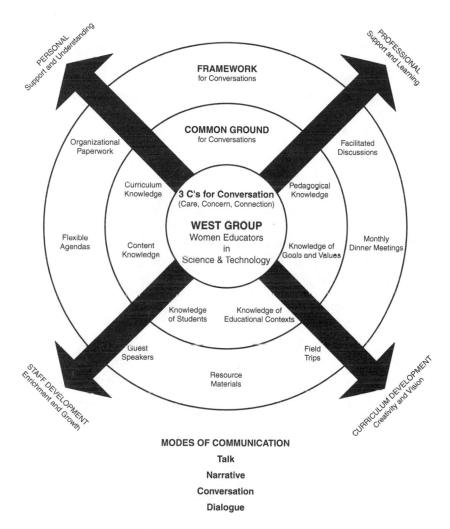

Figure 7.1. Teacher conversations as opportunities for learning and development.

members of the conversation group need to have a genuine respect for one another's opinions; otherwise the voices will go unheard. Knowing the other members care about your life and your teaching makes it safe to tell your story.

Concern is a deeper level of care with commitment. When we feel concern for someone in our group, we are willing to invest time to help them. For example, when April started teaching physical science, she lacked confidence and experience because her background was in biology. Marilyn, who has a strong background in physics, was willing to meet with April to show her useful activities and clarify concepts. With just caring, Marilyn would be empathetic to April's situation but not obligated to help. With concern, she is committed to supporting April in her efforts to find a solution. It is necessary for members of the conversation group to have concern for one another because personal support promotes growth.

Connections are formed as members share experiences. When a conversation group first forms, there may not be many connections. However, as the group talks and shares experiences together, connections are formed. For example, in the spring of 1998, WEST developed a county-sponsored curriculum grant. It was in the process of writing the grant, building display boards, and attending the award banquet that memories were created and connections built within our group.

Middle Circle: Common Ground

Multiple connections, beyond shared experiences, exist among the women of WEST because the younger teachers, along with Lynne and Melissa, have explicitly committed themselves to the goal of the UCSB Teacher Education Program. This goal is to "prepare teachers to learn from their teaching so they can, during their preparation and throughout their careers, become the teachers that students and families deserve" (UCSB Teacher Education Program, 1999, p. 1). Consequently, we have a strong philosophical "common ground," which reminds us all that the work of teaching requires perpetual learning.

It is highly significant that the WEST group is composed entirely of women educators of science. This simple fact entails so much because of what it means to be a teacher, a woman, and a scientist. Betsy illustrates how our common ground maps on to Shulman's (1987) categories of teacher knowledge:

> *Knowledge of Goals and Values.* With those who know your line of work and understand the relevant parts of your job, the fundamentals are presumed and more time can be spent discussing important and pressing issues. We can give each other advice because we have experienced similar situations. In the WEST group, we often discuss the political aspects of our teaching because we know

California's legislative decisions will directly affect us professionally. We take the time to educate each other on new legislation
and keep up-to-date on local and county initatives and mandates
that will impact classroom teaching and learning.

Content and Curricular Knowledge. In our monthly meetings, we
share lesson plans since we all teach in the domain of science. Although it is possible to talk with teachers outside the discipline of
science about general educational topics, discussions about setting
up and taking down labs for well over 150 students each day do
not mean as much to a math or English teacher. An English
teacher may tell you to put in more reading and writing, and a
math teacher suggests incorporating more calculations and graphs,
but a science colleague can help you create and implement more
creative ways to engage students in science. WEST members have
similar goals, which helps us share ideas about how to provide
challenging, innovative science content at low monetary cost.

Knowledge of Educational Context. Although women have made
significant strides in the field of science in the latter half of this
century, there are still barriers to cross and walls to break down.
Several of us in WEST continue to deal with sexism on the job.
We help each other find ways to deal with these problems and
explore possible solutions. Our problems often involve male colleagues and administrators not taking us seriously as leaders
within our departments. We are treated as beginners who need
someone to "fix" our situations rather than work with us as colleagues.

Pedagogical Knowledge. It is easy for us to share our lesson
plans because we have common pedagogical ways of teaching.
Since most of us went through the same credential program, we
were all introduced to similar strategies focused on meeting the
needs of all students. We share the idea that hands-on learning is
the best way for our students to learn. By doing the science themselves, the students come to see science as an inquiry-based discipline. They learn to pose questions and find ways to answer their
own questions rather than relying on a teacher to construct their
knowledge of science.

Knowledge of Learners. The WEST group has a shared knowledge of learners since we all teach at middle–senior high schools
in Santa Barbara and Ventura Counties. Not only do we teach similar age groups, but we all have diverse populations of students
ranging from fluent English speakers to those who are learning the
English language for the first time, from high socioeconomic back-

grounds to those who live in homeless shelters and in need of federal and state support. This commonality helps us to collect and share curricular materials for all of our students.

Outer Circle: Framework

Ongoing conversations occur when a framework is in place that brings us together for meaningful and worthwhile opportunities to talk and share. The framework for the WEST group includes specific organizational strategies that are consistent and firmly in place, while allowing for flexibility and adaptability. The framework for the group has evolved over time and we hope the following descriptive overview will provide readers with the necessary ingredients to establish other conversation groups, in different contexts and with different goals and experiences.

Conversations can take place anywhere, in any type of setting. We believe, however, that a framework is essential if a group hopes to create a stable and safe environment for free-flowing talk. Marilyn provides this overview of the WEST framework:

Monthly Dinner Meetings. The first component of our framework is the monthly dinner meeting. We schedule our meetings a month apart so the timing does not infringe upon participants' personal lives but is frequent enough so that discussions are not forgotten. The meetings take place at the homes of the participants. The evening is thus spent in a warm and safe environment with few distractions allowed. The dinner provides a practical reason for gathering, and food is a wonderful conversation starter. It transcends all barriers, cultural and personal, and satisfies a basic need. Once participants are full, the general mood of the group is more relaxed. Also, sharing food preparation chores allows the participants to feel they have contributed to the evening's events.

Flexible Agendas and Organizational Paperwork. Tied into the dinner meetings are the flexible agendas and organizational paperwork that help bring the meetings into existence. Time is set aside during each meeting to plan future gatherings. With a group of five or more, participants must be flexible so dates can be agreed upon. Once the dates for meetings are set, paperwork must be regularly sent out reminding participants of the date, location, and agenda for the upcoming meeting. This is an important matter, especially for teachers who are inundated with meetings.

Facilitator. A facilitator gently guides the discussion along the agenda to ensure that progress is made on current projects. In our

group, Lynne serves as the facilitator and is responsible for send-
ing out the monthly reminders and organizing the potluck dinners.

Guest Speakers, Resource Materials, and Field Trips. Once the dinner meetings are established and well attended, guest speakers, resource materials, and field trips can be introduced to provide
unique opportunities for shared experiences. These experiences
serve to further strengthen the bonds between group members.

An effective framework requires consistent and proper mainte-
nance by all members of the group. By paying attention to the various components of our framework, we have created a safe and stable environment in which conversations can flow.

ARROWS OF GROWTH

Four modes of communication—talk, narrative, conversation, and dialogue—occur throughout our conversations and provide opportunities
for learning and growth in four major areas: personal, professional, curriculum development, and staff development. Four arrows, representing the
types of teacher learning, cut through the concentric circles in our model
and indicate a conversational pathway, which extends from the core
elements of care, concern, and connection outward through our common
ground and established framework. The arrows point outward from the
center because we believe profound, long-range growth occurs only when
the core elements, the three C's, are well developed and strong. Without
the core elements, personal, professional, and political aspects of our work
cannot be made public and safely discussed in an open forum.

All of the women of WEST are members of school or college departments that possess many of the components of common ground and a
framework for efficiently dealing with required meetings. Our collective
experience demonstrates, however, that departmental groups do not
spend time cultivating the three C's of care, concern, and connection, as
WEST does. Departments offer resources, information, curricular materials, and perhaps opportunities for professional growth. In a well-function-
ing department, we believe it is possible for a teacher to achieve growth
in two or possibly three of the types of teacher learning, but rarely all
four. The culture of science and the nature of science departments are
not conducive to nor do they promote personal growth.

From the multitude of examples we have to draw from over the past
3 years, we have chosen to highlight five stories to illustrate how WEST has
provided opportunities for growth and learning. Each story demonstrates

how, for women science teachers, the personal is professional is political (Keller, 1985).

Area One: Personal Growth

Personal growth is a form of inner growth that involves an increased awareness of self related to individual needs, values, and beliefs. The growth often leads the individual to experience a change of perspective and new ways of thinking about self and others.

WITH A LITTLE HELP FROM MY FRIENDS (BETSY)

Three years ago, I joined WEST because I felt it was a place to get lesson plans, figure out how to make my science classes more female-friendly, and get advice about professional issues that I encountered. I soon discovered that WEST was all this and more. It did not take us long to establish good friendships and I look forward to our monthly meetings. It was in my third year of teaching (and of being a member) that I discovered how much I needed WEST. Early in my third year, my father passed away. I was gone from school for a week and when I came back, I had a hard time adjusting. This was partially due to being gone during the crucial ground rule-setting time for my classes and partially due to not being in a good state of mind. I was having a hard time disciplining my classes and I noted that I just did not feel the same about my profession. Mondays usually went well for me. Tuesdays were hard to get through, but I thought I would teach another 5 years. Wednesdays were much tougher and I figured I would teach through the end of the school year. Thursdays, I felt I would teach through the semester, but by the end of the day on Fridays, I seriously considered turning in my resignation the following Monday morning.

The WEST group had a meeting at the beginning of November, about a month and a half after my father passed away. I shared with them my feelings about not wanting to teach anymore. They were all sensitive to what I was going through and the frustration I was feeling. We spent half the meeting that night discussing my personal/professional problems. While discussing my issues, they helped me to realize that my feelings about teaching were based primarily on what happened with my father and that I would eventually be motivated to teach again.

I didn't go back to school the next day after that WEST meeting feeling completely regenerated, but it was a turning point for me. I started to feel a little more positive about my career. At several meetings throughout the rest of the year, someone would always ask how I was doing and if things were going better. I remember a meeting in February where we talked a little more in-depth about my situation. The WEST group helped me to see that when you are in the midst of a crisis, it helps to have someone not involved in the crisis help ground you. That is what WEST did for me. The year progressed slowly for me, but I was recovering.

Although I still feel the effects of my father's passing, I am getting ready for my fourth year of teaching, and I am excited about it. I am looking forward to trying new things. I am also looking toward having a better year of teaching, thanks greatly to WEST.

Area Two: Professional Growth

Professional growth is focused on what it means to be a professional educator and a learner. Shulman's (1987) categories of knowledge provided a context for the many forms of growth experienced by practicing teachers: the ability to communicate effectively, to be a colleague and a leader, and to deal with the social and political nature of schools and schooling.

THE FRAGMENTED SCIENCE DEPARTMENT (MARILYN)

Going to the WEST meetings became a habit. But our first few meetings were frustrating to me. I expected to come away from each session with something concrete, a new lesson, a book, or some sort of resource I could readily use in my classroom. But each time, I came away empty-handed. It seemed as though we talked about lessons, books, and resources, but I had nothing to show for all the talk. When Lynne suggested we work on a group project and possibly publish our results, I was at once excited and worried. As a group we were all so different—different teaching styles, different personal backgrounds, different ages and years of experience. How would we work as a group? It took us hours of conversation to decide on a topic. And yet, somewhere along the way, going to the meetings became a habit for me.

So what changed? I think we all changed. Initially we met because of what we had in common. We were all science teachers, female science teachers to be exact, and we were all affiliated with the UCSB's Teacher Education Program in one way or another. This was our common ground. However, this common ground was not enough, in itself, to bring us together as a group. Our monthly dinner meetings provided us with an arena. These dinners, in which much planning and coordination took place, served as the initial framework to get our conversation started. It is always easy to talk about food, and during these dinners, the connections between us grew. It did take time. Once our friendships solidified, I wanted to attend the meetings. I no longer expect material results, but from every meeting I carry away a certain "confidence," a feeling that I belong to a group of thoughtful professional teachers and that I am heard and respected.

Much has happened in my professional and personal life since we started WEST. In the first 2 years of my teaching career, I struggled with a fragmented science department and, in particular, an obstinate veteran teacher who bullied the department chair and rest of us into submission. The entire departmental schedule was formed around this teacher. All materials were suddenly this teacher's possessions. As a new teacher, I decided it was best not to make waves, even though each confrontation was frustrating and resulted in hours of tirades and anger for me afterward at home. The WEST meetings were a good outlet for these tirades. It was a safe forum. The members were not only sympathetic, but because they were removed from the conflict, they were able to be helpful by giving different perspectives or suggesting alternative approaches to dealing with my obstinate veteran colleague. Often it was nice just to be able to tell someone about my problems.

During my third year as a teacher, I became the department chair. Now my role was very different but I found that the problems still existed. Our department still formed our schedule around this teacher, but the other teachers in the department helped shoulder the burden this time and I felt there was more unity within the department. Once again, the WEST meetings were helpful in giving me the confidence I needed to put forth my ideas to department members. I could also learn about how other science departments (seven different schools are represented in WEST) were run and the strategies that worked and did not work. Eventually, our science department began working as a team. Under the rough exterior, the veteran teacher was a wise person. We finally reached a middle ground, mutually agreed upon, so we could work together. Had it not been for the support of various people and the WEST group, I would not have seen the big pic-

ture and would not have been able to forge such a relationship
with this teacher.

Although the WEST group is not my only form of support, it
is an important source of guidance and resourcefulness. Through
WEST, I am consoled, challenged, inspired, outraged, encouraged,
and informed. I meet with a group of women with whom I feel
comfortable and I like this habit we have created.

Area Three: Staff Development

Staff development, often referred to as professional development, relates
to opportunities for enrichment. These opportunities include workshops,
seminars, summer institutes, and coursework, and assist teachers in ac-
quiring new teaching strategies, skills in utilizing new materials and
equipment, and opportunities to work with local, state, and national
resources and resource specialists.

SHARING LIFE EXPERIENCES (MELISSA)

Conversation groups can be a useful form of staff development.
As part of our conversations, we have introduced each other to different science conventions, conferences, institutes, and research opportunities. We receive many brochures for staff development in
our mailboxes at school, but it is difficult to know which will be
valuable and worth the time and money. Having colleagues discuss their experiences at various conferences and institutes saves
time and helps us to get the most out of the ones we attend.

Many of the women in WEST attended UCSB to earn their
teaching credential. During the program, the science student teachers go, as a group, to the California Science Teachers Association
Conference. WEST has continued this tradition. When we hear that
the conference is approaching, we organize transportation and
lodging and decide on what sessions to attend together. We let
each other know which sessions were worthwhile and which ones
to avoid. We often go to different sessions and share the activities
and resources at the next WEST meeting. Knowing there are
friends at a large state convention makes it more comfortable.
When wandering around in a sea of strangers, it is a relief to see a
friendly, familiar face.

Attending conferences, conventions, and institutes together
builds the connections that strengthen the care and concern we

have for each other. It is not just sharing of lessons and activities, but sharing of life experiences. It is staying in a hotel room together, taking the subway or tram, running from session to session, finding the best, most reasonably priced restaurants within walking distance, and discussing relationships.

Area Four: Curriculum Development

Curriculum development involves opportunities for teachers to expand their content-based learning, specifically as it relates to national, state, and local initiatives and demands. The current emphasis on content standards and student achievement requires teachers to assess their existing courses of study and make adjustments that will enhance learning and achievement by all students.

FINDING A COMMON THREAD (DEBBY)

In the beginning, WEST was a way to reconnect with my roots in the teaching profession and a way to maintain contact with Lynne. She was someone I respected and trusted both as a supervisor and as a science educator while in the credential program at UCSB. Our meetings served as an opportunity to share stories of struggles and successes with other science teachers. The stories led to our more formal and facilitated discussions that were more philosophical and intellectual in nature. The drive home after meetings was a time for reflection on both the meeting and the job I was doing in my classroom. I always came away with a sense of renewal and optimism. Telling my story allowed me the opportunity to organize, clarify, and simplify the scenario for others as well as for myself.

At times, however, the drive seemed a bit much just for "storytelling." We were all busy and as a group we seemed to be wanting something more. We needed something tangible to rationalize time spent at meetings. We wanted to know the purpose of our meetings and what we were about. We thought we needed a product to show for all the "chatter," and Lynne suggested we come up with a project that could involve everyone.

Development of an integrated aquarium-based science curriculum would serve as our project. It provided a common thread weaving our meeting agendas together and giving us a purpose. There were brainstorming sessions; we had a guest speaker from

Marineland Inc. who spoke with us about other possibilities; and one meeting was held at the Marineland Inc. industrial facility where we toured the facility and received filtration systems for our classrooms.

The project never fully matured as we had envisioned, for a variety of reasons, but it served as an important step for me regarding curriculum development. Through our project conversations and brainstorming, I became aware of Ventura County's Impact II Grants awarded for innovative curriculum. As a result, I submitted applications for and received two grants for curriculum that can now be accessible to other teachers on the Internet. The recognition was nice, but what was most valuable to me was the recognition and show of support from the business community. I felt like my job was important, that people did care, and that going beyond the textbook-driven curriculum was as important in theory as it was in practice.

Whether the aquarium project itself is considered a success or failure, it opened doors to professional opportunities involving curriculum development. As for WEST, it was *our* project and played a valuable role in helping us learn something about ourselves as a group. Along the way we discussed curricular issues, made personal connections, shared more stories, and realized that we did not need a project to define who we were or give value to the group. We agreed that we will continue to work on projects but know that the value of the group lies in something less tangible than a lesson plan or curriculum.

Learning in Multiple Domains

This final story from Adela illustrates how a conversation group can provide the essential elements for growth in all four areas: personal, professional, staff development, and curriculum development.

BROADENING MY HORIZONS (ADELA)

Initially I thought of belonging to this group as a short-term commitment, meeting a couple of times for maybe a year. We were to exchange ideas about teaching and follow a monthly agenda. The first few meetings I was too uncomfortable to share samples of work, or to contribute much to the group. What I found instead was a treasure trove full of ideas for me to try in my classroom. And when I did have problems at school with either my students or my colleagues, this group provided people to really listen to me and sometimes offer advice. I didn't realize how important the group had become both professionally and personally.

Professionally, WEST helped me look at situations from more than my own vantage point. They also helped me grow by sharing common frustrations, like surviving lack of lab supplies, sharing classrooms, or dealing with unruly students. The group provided support by sharing strategies to cope with some of the day-to-day problems. I have come to accept this group as a replacement for a dysfunctional science department at my school. Although my contributions may be few at WEST meetings, I am a part of a team where my voice can be heard free of criticism. The range of teaching settings represented in WEST varies greatly in subject matter and grade level, but we all have common goals for all our students "to be lifelong learners" and that common thread bonds us and keeps us united in our efforts. In the area of curriculum development, I have learned to work collaboratively with people outside of my specific teaching area. I have been introduced to great physics lessons, life science lessons, and integrated approaches to the teaching of science that combine all of the disciplines of science. I have learned to expand ecology to include a unit on fish and have a tank with living fish in my classroom for student observations. After hearing about Debby's creative project with tie-dyeing, I have taken my unit on astronomy and included a section on light, the spectrum, and color. I was able to incorporate tie-dyeing T-shirts into the unit. I have not found opportunities to use all of the curricular ideas we have shared within WEST, but I do keep them on file for future use with my students and with other teachers.

Personally, I found a group of women who could be my friends. We have come together now for 3 years and we have witnessed marriages and new babies alike. Our meetings have evolved away from a set agenda with action items and time limits, to a very casual meeting often started by sharing stories and laughing a lot. I have come to enjoy this part of the meeting the most, and I have found that without Lynne as our facilitator we would just chat the evening away having fun.

Looking ahead, I have no idea what projects we will pursue in the future, or who will be actively involved in the conversations. I do know it is definitely going to be an adventure, full of laughter and sorrow, sharing and talking, learning and growing.

TEACHER TALK: TALK, NARRATIVE, CONVERSATION, AND DIALOGUE

The data for this chapter come from the monthly conversations of the WEST group. For the past 3 years, all of the conversations have been taped to record our various forms of teacher talk. Practically speaking, all of the communication that occurred during our monthly conversation group meetings could be classified as talk. We believe, however, that we participated in four distinctly different forms of teacher talk and that each has a specific purpose and quality of learning associated with it.

In 1998, Alison Cook-Sather of Bryn Mawr College described four modes of communication that we have found useful in distinguishing the types of talk occurring within our WEST conversations (personal communication, July 17, 1998). The four modes of communication (talk, narrative, conversation, and dialogue) occur throughout our meetings; we move from one mode to another and back again with fluidity and ease. Our conversations resemble "women's talk" in the sense that we freely interject ideas, opinions, supporting comments, and advice as a meeting unfolds. A story started by one of us would evolve into a shared collective story that included bits and pieces of others' stories created during the collaborative process. Our conversations have a "spirit of their own" (Gadamer, 1982), and participants do not direct the conversation, but rather are led by the topic or story being shared.

The following descriptions show how we distinguish each form of talk, and selected excerpts from a meeting held in February 1997 demonstrate each form of talk. We selected excerpts from this meeting because the topics of conversation centered around gender, equity, and exploring alternative views of science.

Talk

Talk consists of the anecdotal stories and snippets shared by teachers in informal contexts for the purpose of sharing frustration, joy, and information. Melissa offers one such example:

> I recently gave my students an assignment where they had to use the library and the Internet to look up information on different scientists who were bacteriologists and virologists. I gave them a list of scientists to choose from. One of the girls in class raised her hand and said that if there is not a woman I can do, I am not doing this assignment. I thought to myself, Lynne is going to kill me. I didn't even think about including women on the list.

This excerpt is an anecdotal story in which Melissa is sharing an event that occurred in her classroom. The event immediately triggers for Melissa thoughts of Lynne because she spends considerable time in the Teacher Education Program focusing on gender equity and women's issues in science. Although Melissa told this story in an amusing manner at our WEST meeting, her ruefulness is evident when she says "Lynne is going to kill me."

Narrative

Narrative is a story a teacher tells that integrates intuition, practical experience, reading, and knowledge acquired through conversations with colleagues, parents, and students. Adela offers her experience in a narrative:

> I can tell you how I am using scientists in the classroom. Once a week, I give my students a homework assignment where they have to select an article to read about a famous scientist and write a summary which includes: who the person is, what significant accomplishments she/he made, and explain five scientific activities the person did to achieve the accomplishments. We do famous women, famous men, and then I have collected articles from teenage magazines that highlight teenagers who have accomplished something significant involving science and math.
>
> One of the teenagers featured was a 14-year-old female who was the vice president of a toy manufacturing company, and she makes $50,000 a year. Another was a teenage boy who started his own lawn mowing company and then he started hiring people until he has a whole factory of people working for him. They are mowing lawns and now all he does is organize it on his computer and he earns $50,000 or $60,000 a year now doing a lawn mowing service.
>
> The students have to start pulling out what is a scientific activity from the description of the accomplishment. For example, we talk about calculating how much lawn mowing time it takes to do one yard, knowing area and volume. They have to pull out the math. Then we talk about whether there is any testing, observing, or figuring that has to be done to run a lawn mowing company.
>
> As a group we learn that mothers and fathers have to be scientists when they are in the kitchen. They have to do observing, mixing preparations, and they have to know when things are done and ready to sample. So my goal this year is to teach each one of them that they too are scientists and they hopefully will come up

with this themselves by the end of the year. So I start with famous men then famous women and finally not-so-famous students.

In this narrative, Adela describes a specific activity she uses with her seventh-grade science students. She uses articles from teenage magazines to demonstrate and promote the idea that teenagers can use scientific skills to accomplish their goals. Her reference to mothers and fathers working in the kitchen highlights her belief that everyone is involved in "doing science" and using the skills of science.

Conversation

A conversation is a highly active and engaged form of talk where participants learn through and from the talk by sharing opinions, ideas, and references. The following excerpt is a representative conversation from one of our monthly meetings:

LYNNE: I think it would be ideal to see what topics are covered in your curriculum and see who is working on experiments or doing research locally that would actually help students see that science is happening locally and people doing research in this area are not just completing weird activities they just thought up.

EVERYONE: Um hum!

LYNNE: Like when you think of physical sciences you talk about Newton as an example of a scientist.

MARILYN: Well, that is because we are on the very basic blocks.

LYNNE: What I was thinking was when you teach about Newton's laws that you might bring in someone who uses Newton's laws in some particular way in their work, as opposed to just studying them as weird laws.

MARILYN: Right!

ERIN: We can show a video of Adela's backyard and fruit rolling down hill.

MARILYN: That's the problem with showing students the latest research. The level of understanding that is necessary to comprehend the information is just way over their heads. So you can make it pretty broad, because Newton's laws are like the basic laws of math. You have to understand the laws before we can go on. So it gets hard to bring in all this other stuff. We all agree that it is hard for them to see this science as personal to them.

LYNNE: Right, Newton is just a name. You don't even know if
Newton was married, at least I don't.

MARILYN: Yes, well actually I do. He was married and divorced
for some time. I found a small article on it once on the side of
a book. So I did a "found poem" on him once and had the students do one too. But it's true you don't see many real people.
What I fear is that these students get this history context
where it's just names. I want to avoid getting into the same
track as history where students feel, "Oh gosh this is just another person."

LYNNE: Right.

BETSY: It would be neat to present a lesson on what a person did
and then bring this person into class so students could talk to
the real person.

EVERYONE: Right.

LYNNE: What an interesting idea to think about. If you think about
a scientist working in the general area of Santa Barbara, you
could talk about the work of the person and how it relates to
the science concepts you are studying. Then the students
could do an experiment or investigation and have the person
actually come in and give more detailed information.

MARILYN: Remember when we were in the Teacher Education Program, we picked a scientist to study and then emulated her or
him in front of the class to help bring the person to life.

Lynne initiated this conversation by suggesting teachers invite actual
scientists into their classrooms. Throughout this conversation, members
are sharing ideas about the pros and cons of introducing students to
current science and scientists. Marilyn is helping the group learn by
sharing information from experience and practice, in the end drawing on
her memory of a powerful preservice teacher education experience.

Dialogue

A dialogue is a conversation directed toward discovery and new understanding, where the participants question, analyze, and critique the topic
or experience. Our dialogues, like the following, tend to focus on curricular
issues based on classroom experiences:

MIKA: One of the things I found interesting was when we were doing Darwinism. We were discussing how he was sent on this
trip by his parents because he was unruly. They were afraid

he was not talented enough to do anything and so for his punishment they put him on a ship because he hated being out at sea. They thought if they sent him out to sea, he would be disciplined when he got back. As it turned out, he comes back and turns out to be this person that we all have to study about.

It was really interesting reading the personal profile because the kids were saying, "Yeah he's cool." They could relate to him. When we just say, "This is Darwin," it confuses them, I think. We need to show them that he had a human side. As opposed to being just a "brainiac."

LYNNE: Which isn't to say that some of these people should still be on a pedestal. It would be nice if it wasn't just men.

ADELA: It's my personal view that there were a lot of women out there that just didn't publish.

ERIN: So they go unheard.

ADELA: Yes

LYNNE: Well, most women got to be the helpers. It was pretty unusual for women to actually get grants. So they are not likely to show up in any readings as famous scientists. Do we want to look at people who are dead, as in historical people, or do we want to look at people more current, and present the kinds of things people are doing currently?

MARILYN: I think a range is good.

LYNNE: You know what I think would be good. Take a historical person like Darwin, and then find out what kinds of things people are still doing in that particular field, based on his work. You never really see that.

MARILYN: That's great, it's like following a string. You start with the initial idea and follow it through to the end, the current research.

ERIN: Speaking about Darwin and what we have locally in Goleta Valley, we have a video tape that talks about the Channel Islands as the North American Galapagos. Basically you see the same patterns of species development on the Channel Islands and there is a whole video tape on it. And it is current from the last 10 years. It's a great idea to bring in this idea of here and now. This person on the video tape is somebody that is in the community.

BETSY: What is the name of the woman geologist at UCSB?

LYNNE: Dr. Tanya Atwater.

BETSY: I showed a whole video on her and I was talking with the

> students about her work. Later on, I met her and I had no
> idea that it was her doctoral work that I was showing to my
> students. So if you were studying earthquakes or plate tecton-
> ics, she would be a great scientist to use. She is really into
> geology!
>
> ERIN: You should bring her into your classes.

This exchange followed immediately after the previous example of conversation. We believe we moved into dialogue at this point because the members of the group are learning about Darwin's experience as an adolescent and considering how it led to his fame and position on a pedestal in science. In contrast, we are analyzing why women who did important work in science do not show up in science textbooks. In our discussion about placing the emphasis on dead, historical scientists versus living, current-day scientists, we begin to critique the traditional represen- tation of science and are discovering ways to build upon the past and connect it to the present. Marilyn's notion of "following a string" demon- strates a new way of representing scientists and scientific discoveries.

DILEMMAS WITHIN CONVERSATION GROUPS

Of the many dilemmas that could arise within conversation groups, we have identified three that are specific to our group. We suspect these three could be common to all conversation groups that are long term. The first dilemma is basic and centers on the challenges involved in bringing new members into an established group. The second is related to establishing priorities and the dilemma women face when they must shift their priorities to accommodate professional and personal demands. The third involves our quandary about adding the fourth C of confronta- tion to the interaction style of the group.

Dilemma 1: Including New Members

Becoming a member of a conversation group can be intimidating and unsettling for a young teacher, especially if she joins a community where participants have an established relationship and style of interaction. Melanie joined the WEST group as a first-year teacher during our second year of existence.

At the time Melanie joined, the group did not discuss the impact of a new member joining our community or whether her presence would affect the three C's already established. We made the assumption that

Melanie's connections to science and to the UCSB credential program would provide sufficient common ground to ensure a smooth and comfortable entry into WEST.

WHAT DOES A PHYSICS TEACHER KNOW ABOUT FISH? (MELANIE)

After I received my credential from UCSB, Lynne suggested that I join a group of women science teachers who had been meeting and had started developing a grant proposal together. I remember I had met a few of the women through my student teaching, but my first visit to a WEST group meeting in someone's home made me a little nervous.

Everyone was friendly, of course, and we had dinner, which helped me to get to know who everyone was. But the conversation was peppered with inside jokes and comments about teachers I didn't know and reminiscing about activities I wasn't involved with. This is all normal and expected when you join a group who have been together for a while. We have all spent an evening with a group of people who all know each other, and as much as they try to be nice, the conversation just seems to exclude us. Another issue that made me feel out-of-place was the science backgrounds of the women in WEST. It seemed to me (though I have learned otherwise since then) that they were all life science types. There was one other physics teacher and the rest were junior high science and biology teachers. I found it difficult to relate to them, even though we were all science majors. I thought this group would help me work on curriculum and plan lab activities, but it didn't seem that anyone was very interested in physics.

The project the WEST group was working on involved starting an aquarium in the classroom, using it to collect long-term data, and conducting experiments with students in the courses they taught. I didn't know anything about fish or what they needed to survive in captivity. I thought, "How can I do this in a physics course?" They all had grand ideas about charting chemical levels and testing dissolved oxygen, developing an entire month-long unit for their classes. I really didn't think I had much to offer, nor did I think I would find the curriculum useful.

It took several months of meetings before the differences in disciplines and grade levels seemed to no longer matter. I found that school issues and professional goals translated across those boundaries and I began to seek advice and counsel from these more experienced women. I also found I was able to offer some of my own ideas and suggestions, even about fish, which made me feel more a part of the group. I spent most of my spring break that year in the university library, researching for the aquarium project and trying to put together curriculum for an integrated science class I was teaching. I think I learned more from that aquarium project than anyone else. I created *and actually used* a large portion of the practical classroom activities that went into that project. Other WEST members helped me troubleshoot when I implemented the unit, and Lynne even came to my classroom to observe its progress. She gave me great insight into some biology activities I could add and experiments that I had not thought of because of my limited life science background. Most of all, I remember the great bonding experience we had putting it all together; our successful and not so successful efforts at setting up the aquariums, keeping our fish alive for more than one day, and managing the uncontrollable algae and snail populations that appeared without warning; and the jokes . . . I'm in on them!

The perspective presented by Melanie in this story causes us to question our original assumption about her ease of transition into WEST. We now wonder if we should have been explicit about the group's framework, goals, and ways of communicating. Would this have allowed Melanie to establish care, concern, and connection more quickly?

Fall 2000 is the first time new teachers will be added to our group since Melanie came. We suspect the impact on the group will be greater this time because three new members at once will join our more established group. Our dilemma involves our ambivalence about introducing the new members to the conversation model presented in this chapter. Should we explain the intricacies of the three C's, the common ground, and the framework, or just let them discover the model for themselves as they interact with members of the group, as Melanie did? We can't impose care, concern, and connection on these women, but we are aware of the importance of these qualities to the life of this group.

Dilemma 2: Balancing the Personal and the Professional

There are times, however, when each member must re-evaluate and decide whether participating in WEST is something she should continue to do. Obligations and responsibilities often arise that conflict with the monthly meeting dates. We are all busy women with personal and professional lives. Several group members have stopped coming to the meetings.

We continue to send them the monthly invitation but we know their priorities have shifted. We asked three of the nonactive members of WEST to share why they are unable to participate. Their stories highlight the challenges of fulfilling multiple roles and being forced to make choices to meet the demands of their personal and professional lives.

TIME CONSTRAINTS (MIKA)

There were great benefits I reaped from the WEST meetings the first year I participated. These benefits included the ability to network with other teachers, to have the opportunity to brainstorm and get fresh ideas, to be able to get collegial support and simply talk, and being a part of a group of educators whom I greatly respected and admired. Despite these wonderful benefits, I encountered obstacles that prevented me from actively continuing to participate in the following year.

First, time became a major factor as my professional career was becoming more and more challenging. During my second year of teaching, I was "blessed" with piloting and implementing the AVID [Advancement Via Individual Determination] program at my school site. This additional responsibility was extremely stressful. I found myself putting in long hours at school, usually arriving on campus by 6:30 a.m. and not leaving until 8:00 p.m. The work that was involved in the implementation of the AVID process spilled over into my home life and I was working madly until midnight, on many occasions, just to catch up on my "regular" responsibilities of lesson planning and grading papers. In general, I was reaching a state of "burnout" and I needed to make a decision for my personal sanity. I simply could not participate at the WEST meetings in the capacity that I wanted. I could attend, but I knew I would not be able to carry out the group projects being proposed.

In addition, by the end of the teaching day, it became extremely difficult for me to even commit to driving to Santa Barbara from Ventura, which was another hour and a half round trip on the road. Instead, with the little time I did have for myself, I committed to doing something I would enjoy and unrelated to education. I started swing dancing. But even the dancing took its toll, requiring me to travel extensively on weekends and on occasion weekdays. For these reasons, I found it difficult to make WEST a priority.

When I look back on my decision, I do not think there was anything that could have alleviated the time constraint—except perhaps rotating the meetings, on occasion, to Ventura so I did not always have to drive to Santa Barbara. Even then, I am not sure I would have been able to carry out the projects the group was working on. I do love meeting with the women of WEST. As my personal work load lightens and I get better with managing my time, I plan to rejoin the group on a more active status. So, keeping the inactive members up-to-date with meeting dates and keeping the membership open is greatly appreciated and a way to get members like myself back into the group.

THE REALITY OF MY LIFE (NEA)

The first time I heard about WEST from Lynne, I was excited and intrigued. I have always enjoyed women's groups as they have been a source of inspiration and support for me on many levels. To create this in the field of science teaching seemed like a great idea.

The reality of my life seemed to keep me from immersing myself fully into WEST. Initially, I lived 50 miles away from the group meetings. Spending 2 hours in the car on a work day was just too much for me. This was compounded by the fact that I became a mother. After moving to Santa Barbara a year ago, I believed that I would finally be able to embrace the group at last. However, it seemed that this was harder to put into action. I would pick up my son at 4:30 p.m., after being away from him for 9 hours and was thrilled to have him near me again. I pictured bringing him to a baby-sitter for another 3 hours away from me. Not a possibility, even if only once a month. I tried bringing him with me to meetings, thinking this would be a good compromise. Instead, it prevented me from really engaging myself with the group and also having to attend to my son's needs. I would leave the meeting thinking that I had no idea what "they" were talking about.

I wish there was a way I could make the meetings work, but at this time in my son's life he is the first and foremost priority, way above and beyond even my teaching. I found that it was too difficult to be away from him and then too difficult to stay in touch with the group's topics.

INVESTING IN MY FAMILY FIRST (APRIL)

For the past year, I have been quite content to forget about the difficult aspects of teaching. I didn't realize how weary I had grown

of a difficult department, and a school that needed many academic, safety, curricular, and facility improvements. These were all
issues that the WEST group helped me to not only tolerate, but
aim to improve according to my personal philosophies and hopes
for education. Returning to the WEST meetings after my daughter
was born reminded me of all the difficult issues—though I enjoyed the friendships of the women immensely. During this season
of my life I need support for different difficult issues like parent-
ing, etc. The thought of mind-, time- and heart-consuming problems is overwhelming because I've decided to invest in my family
first. I really do care about these important educational problems,
and I wonder how they will work into my life later. I really appreciate Lynne and the group's willingness to accept me in this
stage of my life and allow me to be minimally involved yet well-
informed. They make me feel like my mind and experience in
education are important, and haven't disappeared with nursing
and changing diapers.

For those who continue to attend meetings, obstacles are overcome
in different ways. To solve day-care problems, Marilyn brings her baby
girl to the first hour of every meeting until her husband travels after work
to whomever's house we are occupying to pick her up. Betsy and Debby
drive at least 60 minutes to get to our meetings . . . after work . . . and
then drive back home at 8 or 9 p.m. Lynne has a multitude of commitments
related to her professional life as a teacher educator. Yet, she carefully
arranges her schedule to allow time for these meetings.

At times, people outside the group question the time commitment
we each have made to WEST. Two of the women's husbands have raised
questions such as, "What do you *do* there?" and "Why are you still going
if you teach health not science?"

We also have to schedule meetings around the events of life, such
as four weddings and four babies. And sometimes attending another
meeting is too much. There is, however, a core of women who consistently
have made the effort to work around their challenging circumstances to
get to the monthly meetings.

Dilemma 3: Collective Problem Solving

The most powerful form of learning, the most sophisticated form of
teacher development, comes not from listening to the good works of others but from sharing what we know with others. . . . By reflecting on what

we do, by giving it coherence, and by sharing and articulating our craft knowledge, we make meaning, we learn.
                                    —Roland Barth, *Improving Schools from Within*

WEST meetings *do* offer this place for sharing, but can they offer more? Is it possible for members to actively challenge each other to deepen reflective thinking and further promote professional growth?

It was the writing of this chapter that led to our discussion of how or even whether we challenge each other. Confrontation is one method for posing a challenge. Our commonly shared understanding of confrontation implies opposition in a hostile manner. For a group in which care, concern, and connection are at the core of the relationship, is it desirable to incorporate confrontation into the three C's? Would the dynamics of the group change? Melissa explained that we "don't confront each other because the relationships are too important!"

Does the lack of confrontation then represent a weakness of our group? Deborah Tannen (1990) explains it not as a weakness, but instead as stylistic, typical of women's conversation. "To most women, conflict is a threat to connection, to be avoided at all costs. Disputes are preferably settled without direct confrontation. But to many men, conflict is the necessary means by which status is negotiated, so it is to be accepted and may even be sought, embraced, and enjoyed" (p. 150).

If this is the case, are there other ways to pose challenges? Lynne is the one person who challenges group members on a regular basis. This seems a natural extension of her supervisory role in the credential program at UCSB. Debby comments on this pattern:

> It is the way that Lynne asks questions that makes her effective at challenging group members without jeopardizing the relationships. She can ask the tough questions without making you feel stupid or belittled. Her questions are phrased in a way that empowers us. She poses her questions as "what ifs" and offers suggestions when sought without jumping in to fix the problem for us. She trusts that we can solve the problem and serves as a dependable resource and caring facilitator. Our relationship is one of cooperative problem solving. I can trust her and in turn can be honest with her and with myself. Lynne is a role model for how to effectively ask the tough questions. We simply need to join her in challenging each other.

For WEST, focusing our attention on developing skills in collective problem solving and continuous inquiry may be a more natural path to deeper thinking and professional growth than introducing confrontation and thereby threatening the core.

CONCLUSION: TAKE MY HAND

In the process of writing this chapter, the women of WEST have come to understand and appreciate how we evolved into an inclusive community of learners and why our "teacher talk" is an empowering and enriching form of professional development. Hours and hours of conversation have gone into the pages of this chapter, and yes, we did confront, challenge, and debate about the components of the model, the stories we chose to share, and the tone and style of our writing. To our amazement, we realize that confrontation can be positive; it can and does force us to be articulate and thoughtful about ourselves as women and our work as scientists and educators.

When the WEST conversation group was organized 3 years ago, our vision was to create an ideal inclusive place for "women's talk" like the one Marni Pearce (1993) describes in her poem: "a place where souls can meet and share and experience and lives can intermingle." At the time, it was not clear how we would create such a place. We just knew in our hearts if the three C's of care, concern, and connection were used as our guiding principles, WEST could be a "haven for all."

Creating a safe space does not, however, mean that everyone invited to join will take the time needed to cultivate the three C's and make the commitment to actively participate, to learn, and to grow in an inclusive community. It is evident from the stories shared by Mika, Nea, and April that life happens and choices must be made to accommodate both personal and professional needs. For the women in WEST who have made the group a priority, opportunities for learning are endless, within the four types of teacher learning identified in our model and beyond. Each of us has found a purpose that makes it possible to overcome obstacles of time, family, schedules, and professional obligations, to benefit from "a smile of recognition, a reassuring touch, a sense of genuine belonging" (Pearce, 1993).

In September 2000, as noted earlier, 3 first-year women science teachers joined WEST. The current members believe we have the capacity to welcome new members into the community and adapt to meet the needs of our younger colleagues. We already "care" about the safety and well-being of these young women entering into the science teaching profession. The more critical issue facing us now is uncertainty about our capacity and their ability to develop a deep concern and strong connections to the women of WEST. We know life is uncertain and priorities cannot be mandated for any member of the group. The best we can do is offer to others this opportunity to learn, to grow, and to be empowered within an inclusive community, and extend our hands to our new members and to each other and "go there together."

NOTE

Contributing members of WEST were Marilyn Garza, Melissa Kehl, Adela Laband, Melanie Pearlman, Mika Shibuya, April Torres, Betsy Villalpando, Andrea "Nea" Voss, and Debby West.

REFERENCES

Barth, R. (1990). *Improving schools from within: Teachers, parents, and principals can make the difference*. San Francisco: Jossey-Bass.

Belenky, M. F., Clinchy, B. McV., Goldberger, N. R., & Tarule, J. M. (1986). *Women's ways of knowing: The development of self, voice, and mind*. New York: Basic Books

Brown, L. M., & Gilligan, C. (1992). *Meeting at the crossroads*. New York: Ballantine Books.

Casey, K. (1993). *I answer with my life: Life histories of women teachers working for social change*. New York: Routledge.

Chambers, C. (1992, November). *Looking for a home*. Paper presented at the eighteenth Annual Conference on Women and Education, Pennsylvania State University, State College, PA.

Connelly, F. M., & Clandinin, D. J. (1990). Stories of experience and narrative inquiry. *Educational Researcher, 19*(4), 2–14.

Gadamer, H. (1982). *Truth and method*. New York: Crossroad.

Gilligan, C. (1982). *In a different voice: Psychological theory and women's development*. Cambridge, MA: Harvard University Press.

Gilligan, C., Lyons, N. P., & Hammer, T. J. (Eds.). (1990). *Making connections: The relational worlds of adolescent girls at Emma Willard School*. Cambridge, MA: Harvard University Press.

Heilbrun, C. G. (1988). *Writing a woman's life*. New York: Ballantine Books.

Hogan, P. (1988). *A community of teacher researchers: A story of empowerment and voice*. Unpublished manuscript.

Keller, E. F. (1985). *Reflections on gender and science*. New Haven: Yale University Press.

Little, J. W. (1990). The persistence of privacy: Autonomy and initiative in teachers' professional relations. *Teachers College Record, 91*(4), 491–517.

Martin, J. R. (1987). Reforming teacher education, rethinking liberal education. *Teachers College Record, 88*(3), 406–409.

Novak, M. (1978). *Ascent of the mountain, flight of the dove* (2nd ed.). San Francisco: Harper & Row.

Pearce, M. (1993). Inclusive communities. *Journal of Among Teachers Community, 10*(1), 1ff.

Rogers, A. G. (1993). Voice, play, and a practice of ordinary courage in girls' and women's lives. *Harvard Educational Review, 63*(3), 265–295.

Schubert, W. H., &. Ayers, W. C. (Eds.). (1992). *Teacher lore: Learning from our own experiences*. New York: Longman.

Shulman, L. (1987). Knowledge and teaching: Foundation of the new reform. *Harvard Educational Review, 57*(1), 1–22.

Tannen, D. (1990). *You just don't understand: Women and men in conversation*. New York: Ballantine Books.

UCSB Teacher Education Program. (1999). *Single subject credential handbook*.

Yocum, M. R. (1985). Woman to woman: Fieldwork and the private sphere. In R. Jordan & S. Kalcik (Eds.), *Women's folklore, women's culture* (pp. 45–54). Philadelphia: University of Pennsylvania Press.

CHAPTER 8

Good Conversation

Christopher M. Clark

W E HAVE LEARNED a great deal about how conversations can become authentic learning experiences for teachers. The work reported here is both about the dynamics of a special kind of talk and about learning—changes in participants' understanding, skill, morale, and dispositions. At the beginning of the parallel adventures described in this book, we shared a hope and a dream that developing and documenting a variety of teacher conversation groups could, just possibly, help us and our colleagues think in constructive and unconventional ways about personal and emotional support for teachers and teacher learning, and that it might give new meaning to the words "sustainable professional development for teachers."

As with all hopes and dreams, what we have realized is more complicated and subtle than we imagined 5 years earlier. We have not discovered or invented one right way to organize teacher professional development. But we have convinced ourselves, and we hope convinced you, that teacher conversation groups constitute a low-cost, sustainable, satisfying, and potentially transformative form of teacher professional development. Our collective experiences put the lie to the cynical view that when teachers have the freedom to talk together, they waste that time on superficial, petty, trivial matters. On the contrary, the common ground that unites

teachers across the spectrum from preschool through high school to graduate school are the mysteries of learning, teaching, and life in all its complex relationships. This closing chapter weaves together our insights and
claims into a lightly held understanding of teacher learning through conversation.

WHAT WE HAVE LEARNED

It would do violence to the individually different testimony of the teachers
whose conversations inform these chapters to analyze their personal-
social-professional-technical-emotional experiences into binary categories
like "process" and "product." Even so, we have seen and heard rich
examples of how teachers transform themselves and attribute the changes
(or their beginnings) to learning conversations. We can go this far, I think:
We can name the variety of changes reported as having been stimulated
by learning conversations, and think of these as opportunities to learn
about our work as teachers and about ourselves in the context of that
work. These are learnings that we have taught ourselves by engaging in
authentic conversation with fellow teachers. These learnings include

- Articulation of implicit theories and beliefs
- Perspective taking: Seeing the world through the eyes of others
- Developing a sense of personal and professional authority
- Reviving hope and relational connection: An antidote to isolation
- Reaffirmation of ideals and commitments
- Developing specific techniques and solutions to problems
- Learning how to engage with students in learning conversations

Articulation of Implicit Theories and Beliefs

Throughout this volume we have read the stories of teachers who have
tried to bring to light and make sense of the deep structures that underlie
their work—the ways in which they interact with their students, the
curricula that they interpret and enact, their attitudes toward authority,
and the ways in which they see themselves in relation to their students,
their colleagues, and their professional community. This is difficult territory and yet, in chapter after chapter, we see evidence that teachers
engaged in professional conversation inevitably move in these directions
when they have had time to get to know one another and to see themselves
as part of a community in which they can care and be cared for. One of
the best ways to come to an understanding of what one believes is to talk

it through with others who understand the challenges of being a good teacher in an uncertain time.

Perspective Taking

The community of the conversation group seems to enable teacher-partici-pants to test their own assumptions and also to see the world through the eyes of others. A learning-oriented conversation, we have discovered, must be open to different, even conflicting, points of view, interpretations, beliefs, and values. Resistance is as important a dynamic in good conversa-tion as is acceptance (Chapter 3). Discussing sensitive "hot lava" topics like racism and sexism calls us on to unfamiliar and even scary ground (Chapter 4). Arab and Jewish teacher mentors moved past stereotypes and assumptions about each other toward sympathetic appreciation of the challenges and possibilities of fulfilling their mentor roles in schools in Israel (Chapter 5). We learned to name what we treasure and what we fear in a struggle with ideas and stories foreign to us. With practice and support we can learn to see the world through the eyes of others quite different from ourselves.

Personal and Professional Authority

In conversation we have come to understand and talk through our individ-ual and collective expertise and, in the process, we have learned how to agree (easy) and to disagree (much harder). This is possible because of an atmosphere of safety, trust, and care, in which there is common ground for discourse. As teachers, each group has found a shared footing. For example, each member of the Santa Barbara conversation group (Chapter 7) can, to some degree, speak with authority about being a female science teacher in a masculine quarter of the profession. And, over time, each member of the Haifa mentors' group (Chapter 5) learned to balance the perspective of a teacher with that of an advisor so that all left the course and the conversation more confident and articulate about their profes-sional roles. Cultivating a sense of personal and professional authority is a special challenge for beginning teachers, and the Bryn Mawr (Chapter 2) and NYU (Chapter 5) group members new to the profession profited hugely in this domain.

Reviving Hope and Relational Connection

Good conversation among these teachers happened on common ground and in an atmosphere of safety, trust, and care. For example, among the prospective and new teachers in the conversation groups at Bryn Mawr (Chapter 2) and at New York University (Chapter 5), a shared teacher education program provided the conversational footing. In others, it was shared concerns such as those felt by the mentors in Israel or the women science teachers in Santa Barbara. Reading and discussing powerful ethnic autobiographies united the Michigan group (Chapter 4). It took time to co-create common ground for the teachers in Lincoln, Nebraska (Chapter 6). Genuine common ground makes full participation possible and enables the development of relational bonds that carry over from one meeting to the next and across a longer arc of time, drawing members back to the conversation if only to be able to talk with one another again and to be reminded by colleagues whose opinions we have come to value of the importance of the work of teaching. Interestingly, very few of the teachers in the conversation groups came from the same school faculties. The conversation groups provided teachers with a network of critical friends who were at once genuinely interested in their stories and working themselves at a discrete distance.

Reaffirmation of Ideals and Commitments

In each of these conversation groups there was and continues to be a deep commitment to education—to teaching and learning—for ourselves as teachers and for our students. The threads of this commitment weave through the conversations. They are there in the discussions of "hot lava" topics like racism and sexism (Chapter 4; Chapter 7), when teachers examine their perspectives and push one another toward emancipatory practice. They are there in discussions of the everyday life of schools (all chapters) as we raise the possibility of more progressive teaching under distressingly constrained circumstances. They are there in our resistance (Chapter 3). Ultimately, these conversations invite recommitment and renewal. In one way or another, they became invitations to reconsider what has become routine, to revivify teacher thought and belief in action.

Developing Specific Techniques and Solutions to Problems

Our conversations show teachers drawing on one another's expertise. Theirs is not idle chatter. It is focused. It is purposeful. It is grounded in commitment to teaching and learning that is remarkable for its pervasiveness and its commonly held assumptions. Each of these groups care deeply about the practice of teaching. Their conversations reverberate with understanding of the uniqueness of each child and a quest to address learners' needs in locally suitable ways. These generative conversations emerged in unpredictable ways and helped participants to articulate tacit assumptions, develop new understandings, and formulate new plans for action. After the groups became comfortable enough to break the common rule of "refraining from advice giving," powerful advice was given and gratefully received, adapted, and taken into action.

Learning to Engage with Students in Learning Conversations

While we have not followed one another systematically into our schools and classrooms, we have heard convincing testimony that these professional conversations among teachers have begun to shape profoundly their practice. Many have been moved to extend their experiences of learning conversations to their students, creating learning communities more generative and empowering than conventional "banking" models of teaching ever can be (Freire, 1970). In the process, these accounts have helped us to identify some of the critical elements of good conversation.

QUALITIES OF GOOD CONVERSATION

The many good conversations described in this volume have a set of common qualities: Good conversations deal with worthwhile content; they resist narrow definition; they are voluntary; they flourish on common ground, in an atmosphere of safety, trust, and care; they develop over time, drawing on a shared history and anticipating a shared future. Conversation group members have formed deeply connected personal and professional relationships and have come to treasure their time together, both as a satisfying end in itself and, more important, as a renewable means to learning and improvement of their effectiveness, satisfaction, and longevity as teachers of the next generation.

Good Conversations Demand Good Content

Good conversations demand good content—something worth talking about; something that every participant can get intense about. Some of the most generative learning conversations in this book began with reading a well-written and provocative book or chapter. Others began with personal stories, reports of adversity endured, heroic teaching, or drama unresolved. Both the exotic and the familiar have held center stage.

Generative conversational content takes many different forms, but all have this in common: Directly or indirectly, what is worth talking about has a personal connection for the conversants. It has to do with their lives, hopes, fears, fascinations, and aspirations. Generative content has another quality: It is content that brought forth animated, learning-oriented conversation. Its emergence is not predictable. Not every promising text or story fulfills its promise, and some of the best conversations came as complete surprises.

Michal Zellermayer (Chapter 3) showed a video of Canadian teachers to a group of Israeli teachers, with the intention of illustrating how writing conferences look. But the Israeli teachers keyed on the apparent wealth of material resources evident in Canadian classrooms compared with their own, and launched a fiery (and partly defensive) conversation about how lack of resources constrain and frustrate them as good teachers.

A paradoxical feature of generative content is that the conversation it sparks is not always *about* the content. The participants are not breaking through to conversation to learn more about *Why the Caged Bird Sings*, or about *Hunger for Memory*, or about how Canadian teachers conduct writing conferences. Rather, teachers used these artifacts as points of departure and connection that invite and inspire conversants to create common ground. Authentic conversation is about making sense of and articulating our own experiences, implicit theories, hopes, and fears, in the intellectual and emotional company of others whom we trust. While some incidental learning about texts and topics may follow from these conversations, the heart of conversational learning for teachers is about ourselves.

Good Conversation Resists the Bounds of Definition

We recognize a good conversation when we are in one, and for a time the glow persists. But we have no guarantee that if we bring the same conversants together again in the same room at the same hour, a second good conversation will follow a first. For teachers intent on bringing conversation into their classrooms, there is always uncertainty. What we know is that good conversation may be invited, never commanded, and that some invitations are more likely to bear fruit than others. The optimistic manner in which we come to the conversation and the stories that we bring are critical.

Good Conversation Is Voluntary

Involuntary conversation, which seems like a contradiction, is either an interrogation disguised, a monologue, or talking in one's sleep. For a conversation to have a chance of getting good, the participants must want to be there, must want to cooperate. We do not think that professional conversations can be required of teachers. Mandated talking, listening to designated authorities, and meeting on another's agenda are not the stuff of generative professional learning or adaptive personal support.

Good Conversation Happens on Common Ground

At the very least, participants in a good conversation share a common language. But this is not enough. Speakers and listeners in a good conversation are usually members of a shared discourse community, using shared vocabulary and register, following unwritten rules about topics, turn taking, and taboo. All these help but are not yet common ground. Values, ideas, fears, and important shared experiences bring us close to what I mean by common ground. WEST (Chapter 7) is composed of women who teach science. As different as their individual lives, stories, joys, and frustrations may be, they share a felt sense of what it is like to live and work in a masculine quarter of the profession. They have a great deal to give and receive from one another, without having to start at square one. Each conversant is, to some degree, a voice of authority on being a female science teacher. This feeling of authority, however tentative at first, works against self-silencing. Genuine common ground makes full participation possible.

Not all talk among people who share common ground and come together voluntarily becomes good conversation. Talk has many forms and functions: practical, instrumental, ritual, entertainment, control, organizing, persuading, connecting, inspiring, arguing, calming, rewarding, punishing, explaining, and informing, to name a few. Each of these could result from or be embedded in a good conversation. But much of what we accomplish through talk does not require good conversation.

Good Conversation Requires Safety, Trust, and Care

Why are these conditions so important? Fully entering into conversation can feel risky and threatening. Conversational engagement invites us to become vulnerable by telling our personal experience stories, taking a position, or expressing opinions, uncertainties, and regrets. Ego and identity are on the table, out from behind the mask of everyday talk. For talk to become good conversation, the participants need to know that exposing their vulnerabilities will not bring judgment, punishment, or rejection.

An atmosphere of safety, trust, and care can be cultivated but not commanded. Meeting in a comfortable place at a comfortable time can help. Coming together in a private home goes a long way toward establishing a safe atmosphere, as does the sharing of food. Especially in the first meetings of a conversation group, articulating and negotiating a simple set of ground rules can provide a safety net. The following four rules have stood the test of time in beginning conversation groups:

1. *No interrupting.* Allow the speaker time, including silence, to say what he or she has to say.
2. *No unsolicited advice giving.* Advice often includes implied judgment and criticism. Allow the speaker to explore and describe the situation without rushing into a problem-solving mode.
3. *"I pass."* Any group member at any time can decline to speak or respond to a question without prejudice by saying "I pass."
4. *Confidentiality.* What is said within the conversation group stays within the conversation group.

At first, abiding by ground rules can seem stilted and constraining, but this soon passes. The enabling conditions of safety, trust, and care are expressed in the manner and tone in which conversants respond to one another, in the mutual trust and respect they show, in connections made and confidences kept.

Agreeable as this sounds, there is a pitfall in paying exclusive attention to safety, trust, and care. A conversation in which everyone is careful to agree with and support everything said is not likely to go forward, to open new possibilities, or to become an occasion for learning. In good conversation we learn to agree to disagree, while sustaining the conversational relationship by much trial and error.

Good Conversation Develops

When groups of teachers have met to talk month after month over several years, their conversations change and develop in regular patterns. Early conversations and the stories told within them establish the identities of the participants and probe the boundaries of spoken and implicit rules of exchange (Chapter 6). Getting comfortable with conversation and with one another is the highest priority, laying the foundation for safety, trust, and care.

As a conversation group develops and participants find their voices, the conversational floor opens to greater complexity, depth, and tolerance of uncertainty. Teachers are more ready to wonder, speculate, think aloud, and express doubt and regret. Thoughtful, supportive listening becomes more important than advice giving or problem solving. Teachers also begin to develop the courage to disagree, while still continuing their mutually supportive relationships.

When a conversation group continues to meet for more than one school year, topics and patterns of talk develop that reflect the annual cycle. Rust and Orland (Chapter 5) persuade us that the annual cycle of teacher conversation can take on an ascending spiral pattern, becoming progressively more complex and sophisticated when re-encountering familiar themes. Further, the momentum of a long-term conversation group is strong enough to carry new members to new heights in a kind of collective assisted performance. The group has learned how to raise the probability of making good conversation happen again and again.

In Israel, when invited to a party, each guest is expected to bring three new stories as a gift to the occasion. As we have seen in this volume, a similar ethos takes hold in a well-developed conversation. Each participant looks for and collects stories, sightings, insights, and wonderings to bring to the table. Like jazz, a good conversation is improvised, but the improvising participants are working with freshly prepared, relevant, and interesting material. Everyone shows up ready to play. Responsibility for beginning and sustaining good conversation is distributed across all members, and leadership becomes collective.

Good Conversation Has a Future

One of the pitfalls of joining a voluntary conversation group is that it can become too comfortable—a place for people on the margin to come together to complain about the unfairness of the system; a place to be comfortable with being stuck. But the successful conversation groups described in this book avoided the trap. These groups each embody a commitment to support better teaching and learning by their members. Good conversation among these teachers became time apart from the daily pressures of teaching, time to make sense of experiences, time to express doubts, beliefs, and new insights to an audience of thoughtful peers. A conversation group, in the best of circumstances, becomes a social context for doing the work of reflective practice. But collective reflection, satisfying as it is, did not become an end in itself. Conversational reflection became a means for organizing ourselves for future action in our classrooms and schools. In this sense, teacher conversation groups can become field-based, self-directed, sustainable extensions of more conventional teacher education and professional development programs.

CONCLUDING THOUGHTS

Every teacher knows that lively, flowing, worthwhile discussion is rare and difficult to achieve. Interesting and invitational questions, put to a class, can die in a room full of silence and averted eyes. Conversation cannot be forced, even by a powerful leader. Conversation is jointly constructed, improvisational, and personally revealing. To achieve and sustain a conversation, everyone must be willing, even eager, to play his or her part.

Because real conversations are not scripted in advance, conversants must be willing to improvise, to listen attentively and empathetically, and to respond in verbal and nonverbal ways that carry the conversation forward. Yet the direction of "forward" is not always clear. Conversation feels more like an exploratory, wandering walk around a mutually interesting place than a direct journey from one point to another. Intuition is as important as intellectual analysis in guiding participants' contributions to a conversation, including the contribution of attentive silence.

Good conversation feeds the spirit; it feels good; it reminds us of our ideals and hopes for education; it confirms that we are not alone in our frustrations and doubts or in our small victories. As a genre for learning and professional development, conversation groups have the wonderful quality of being controlled by the participants. Professional autonomy tastes especially sweet in a time of standards, accountability, high-stakes testing, mandated teach-to-the-test curricula, and top-down imposition of business models of administration and control on teachers and children. Familiar patterns of teacher professional development (e.g., half-day, decontextualized, canned presentations by traveling experts) simply do not promote long-term, locally relevant, developmentally appropriate learning and support for teachers. Conversation groups give us teachers a room of our own.

And when is a good conversation over? This too can remain uncertain until the moment it ends or is interrupted. So the participants in an authentic conversation must be willing to tolerate uncertainty, to listen attentively and empathetically, to improvise in ways that keep the conversation alive, and often to reveal for the first time their own thoughts, beliefs, opinions, and doubts about the shifting collage of topics in the air. Authentic conversation, like teaching in our best moments, invites a rare kind of intellectual, emotional, and rhetorical group performance, never twice the same.

In *The Courage to Teach*, Parker J. Palmer (1998) reflects on the richness we have come to know directly and commend to you:

> Conversation among friends has its own rewards: in the presence of our friends, we have the simple joy of feeling at ease, at home, trusted and able to trust. We attend to the inner teacher not to get fixed but to befriend the deeper self, to cultivate our sense of identity and integrity that allows us to feel at home wherever we are. (p. 32)

REFERENCES

Freire, P. (1970). *Pedagogy of the oppressed.* New York: Herder & Herder.

Palmer, P. J. (1998). *The courage to teach: Exploring the inner landscape of the teacher's life.* San Francisco: Jossey-Bass.

About the Editor and the Contributors

Christopher M. Clark is Director of the School of Education and professor of education at the University of Delaware. From 1976 to 2000 he was professor of educational psychology at Michigan State University, doing research on teacher thinking, planning, and decision making and written literacy, and working with preservice and experienced teachers. He has been a Fulbright senior research fellow and received awards from the American Educational Research Association for original research and for relating educational research to the practice of teaching and teacher education. He holds a B.S. in social studies from Villanova University, and M.A. and Ph.D. degrees in educational psychology from Stanford University. His book *Thoughtful Teaching* was published by Teachers College Press in 1995.

Lynne Cavazos is Coordinator of the Single Subject Teacher Credential Program and a science education instructor at the University of California, Santa Barbara. She also acts as Director of the Santa Barbara County Beginning Teacher Support and Assessment Program (BTSA) and works as a member of the Science Education Outreach Team for the Materials Research Laboratory at UCSB. Lynne received a B.A. in biology and a secondary teaching certificate from Michigan State University, a master's degree in science education from the University of Michigan, and a Ph.D. in teacher preparation and staff development from Michigan State University. Her research interests include issues of gender and ethnicity in science education, design and implementation of effective professional development programs for science teachers, and support and assessment of beginning teachers.

Alison Cook-Sather is assistant professor of education and Director of the Bi-College Education Program at Bryn Mawr and Haverford Colleges. She holds a B.A. in English literature from the University of California at Santa Cruz, a master's in English education from Stanford University, and a Ph.D. in reading, writing, and literacy from the University of Pennsylvania. Her research interests focus on collaboration in teacher preparation and specifically how to include high school student perspectives in the preparation and professional development of teachers. She has co-edited a volume with Jeffrey Shultz entitled *In Our Own Words: Student Perspectives on School.*

Susan Florio-Ruane is a professor of teacher education at Michigan State University. She has conducted research projects on "Schooling and the Acquisition of Written Literacy," "Autobiographies of Education and Cultural Identity: Preparing Teachers to Support Literacy Learning in Diverse Classrooms," "Reading Culture in Autobiography: The Education of Literacy Teachers," and, with Dr. Taffy Raphael, "Re-engaging Low Achieving Readers: Collaborative Research on the Role of Technology in Teachers' Development of Literacy Curriculum." Her paper on what beginning teachers need to know about "The Social Organization of Classes and Schools" won the 1990 Division K Research in Teacher Education Award of the American Educational Research Association. She served as President of the Council on Anthropology and Education and Associate Editor of *Anthropology and Education Quarterly.* She is author of the forthcoming book *Teacher Education and the Cultural Imagination: Autobiography, Conversation, and Narrative.*

Lily Orland is a junior lecturer at the Faculty of Education, University of Haifa, Israel. Her two main professional and research foci are mentoring and mentored learning, and second language teacher education, in both preservice and inservice education. She holds a B.A. in English language and literature from the University of Haifa, an M.A. in teaching English as a second language from the University of Reading, England, and a Ph.D. in education from the University of Haifa. She has been the leader of numerous inservice projects and professional development frameworks for teachers and mentors in Israel.

Taffy E. Raphael is professor in the Department of Reading and Language Arts at Oakland University, Rochester, MI. She received the Outstanding Teacher Educator in Reading Award from the International Reading Association in May 1997. Dr. Raphael's research has focused on innovations in literacy instruction and in teachers' professional development, and has been published in journals such as *Reading Research Quarterly, Research in The Teaching of English, The Reading Teacher,* and *Language Arts.* She has co-authored and edited several books on research and practice in literacy instruction. She currently serves as president of the National Reading

Conference, and as Associate Director of Research for the Center for the Improvement of Early Reading Achievement.

Frances Rust is associate professor and Director of Undergraduate Programs in the Department of Teaching and Learning at New York University. She is the winner of the 1985 American Educational Research Association Outstanding Dissertation Award. Her research and teaching focus on teacher education and teacher research. Her most recent books are *Changing Teaching, Changing Schools: Bringing Early Childhood Practice into Public Education* (1993, Teachers College Press) and *What Matters Most: Improving Student Achievement*, a volume of teacher research co-edited with Ellen Meyers as part of her work as advisor to the National Teacher Policy Institute, Teachers Network. Recent articles on teaching and teacher education have appeared in the *Journal of Early Childhood Teacher Education, Social Science Record, Journal of Teacher Education, Teaching and Teacher Education*, and *Education Week*. She served as Associate Director of the Preservice Program at Teachers College, Columbia, Director of the Department of Teacher Education at Manhattanville College, and Chair of the Department of Curriculum and Teaching at Hofstra University. She is currently the president-elect of the National Association of Early Childhood Teacher Educators.

Stephen A. Swidler is assistant professor in the Center for Curriculum and Instruction at the University of Nebraska–Lincoln. He teaches courses in the social foundations of education and qualitative research methods for the Qualitative and Quantitative Research Methods in Education program. A former elementary and French teacher and social worker, he earned his doctorate in curriculum, teaching, and educational policy at Michigan State University. In addition to teacher development and the personal experience narrative, his research interests include Nebraska's remaining one-teacher schools. His work has appeared in *Qualitative Studies in Education, Midwestern Folklore*, and *Journal for Research in Rural Education*.

Michal Zellermayer is chair of the Literacy Education Program and coordinator of the M.Ed. program at Levinsky College of Education in Tel Aviv, Israel. She has been a lecturer in the School of Education at Tel Aviv University, where she taught undergraduate and graduate courses in literacy and reading. She has been a visiting scholar at Michigan State University. Her recent publications describe spaces she has designed for authentic conversation among teachers, among children, between teachers and children, and between teachers and researchers. This work has appeared in journals including *Instructional Science, Poetics, The Journal of*

Pragmatics, Teaching and Teacher Education, The Journal of Education for Teaching, Teachers and Teaching, Linguistics in Education, American Educational Research Journal, and *Curriculum Inquiry.* She received her Ph.D. in communication arts and sciences from the School of Education at New York University. Her current research interests include efforts to enhance thoughtful teaching and teacher education and to design with teachers rich communicative environments for teaching literacy.

Index